Unfamiliar Stories of Familiar Hymns

by

WILLIAM J. HART, M.A., D.D.

Member of The Hymn Society of America

With a Foreword by

PHILIP S. WATTERS

President of
The Hymn Society of America

JACKET BY
HAROLD J. CUE

Boston   W. A. WILDE COMPANY   Mass.

Dedicated
to
THE HYMN SOCIETY OF AMERICA

FOREWORD

CHRISTIAN hymns are nearly as old as the Christian Church. Indeed some of our most beloved hymns are still older, for they are translations from the Psalms of the Old Testament. But there is a new interest in hymns and in their stories and in the more formal study of hymnody. This is evidenced by the great number of hymnals and books of hymnology produced within a generation. In our own country this movement has been coincident with a new interest in worship. Nearly all of the important studies in worship produced in the United States have been written within the past twenty years.

Yet there is room for this, another book, for it presents "unfamiliar stories" of the hymns people are fond of singing. Gospel songs as well as hymns are included in these studies. This does not mean that they are of equal literary merit or of equally lasting worth. With this question the present volume is not concerned. The author has performed a labor of love in collecting both published and unpublished material, from all kinds of sources, illustrative of the influence of hymns and gospel songs in the lives of many people. Interesting stories are told concerning the hymns used on a number of historic occasions.

Those who wish to increase the interest in hymns and to make the hymns more meaningful will find these pages of much value and of practical usefulness. Those planning hymn services will be grateful to the compiler of this material.

The great hymns, which follow the Church through the years, are not only a great heritage but a great unifying force. Whatever helps us to appreciate their majesty and appropriate their spirit is to be counted as a very means of grace. Therefore we are especially happy to welcome this volume which speaks a note of triumph in a day of conflict and of fears.

PHILIP S. WATTERS.

White Plains, New York

TABLE OF CONTENTS

INTRODUCTION

THE stories in this volume indicate how hymns relate themselves to life. Old memories are often awakened by the use of a hymn in the home or at a public gathering. Sometimes emotions are deeply stirred as a hymn is quoted or sung. Occasionally something unexpected happens, and the hymn makes the day memorable.

These stories have been gathered from many sources. Some of them have come out of the experiences of the author. Carefully they have been selected from articles in newspapers and religious periodicals where reference has been made to the use of a hymn under unusual circumstances, and the effect it has produced. Books, especially biographical works, have made an enriching contribution to this collection. Sources of the material in the volume are usually indicated in connection with the story. The author has expended considerable effort in the attempt to verify all incidents recorded, and sometimes extensive correspondence has been involved in the effort to be assured of the veracity of a single story. The stories are from both American and British sources.

This book does not deal with music, but with words of hymns. Hence hymn tunes are seldom mentioned. Very little is said about the origins of hymns, and then only when something unusual is associated with the writing of the hymn which is not generally known. When details, however, have been given, the author has consulted many of the foremost authorities to assure the correctness of his statements. " A Dictionary of Hymnology " by Dr. John Julian, to which all writers on hymn subjects are indebted, has often been a source of reference. Two recent works have been particularly useful. These are " Handbook to the Hymnal " by Covert and Laufer (Presbyterian Board of Christian Education); and " Our Hymnody " by Robert Guy McCutchan (The Methodist Book Concern). " The Evolution of the English Hymn " by Frederick John Gilman (Allen & Unwin, London) has also been greatly helpful. Various other works are mentioned in connection with separate stories.

Though each story is complete in itself, and is given a distinctive heading, yet the stories are grouped into chapters. The first line of each hymn used is quoted in the Table of Contents. The persons who use the book can therefore, in a few seconds, ascertain what particular hymns are included in the volume.

Ministers and workers in Christian organizations will here find enough material in each chapter for one or more services. Furthermore, these incidents will suggest others which have come from their own experiences, and can thus be used in connection with those found in the book. An effective method is to relate the story, and then have the hymn sung, either as a solo, by the choir, or the entire assembly. When thus used, the story and the hymn are linked together, and thus form a lasting association. Young people are particularly fond of good hymn stories when used in connection with their " hymn sings." Hymn festivals are very popular in many churches, and this book supplies good material to be used on such occasions. The devotional value of hymns is increasingly recognized, and this volume will, therefore, have value for many individuals for devotional reading. It is, also, what a nurse once characterized as a "bedside book." By this she explained that her life was spent with the sick. Such people, she intimated, often wanted a book from which they could read just a page or two, and then lay it down for future use without having to think of the connection with earlier pages.

The author is greatly indebted to the Rev. Philip S. Watters, an eager student of hymnology, and formerly an instructor in hymnology at Drew Theological Seminary, who examined the manuscript of this work, and who graciously consented to write the Foreword.

Nearly all the selections used, as indicated in the title, are "familiar hymns," and are therefore found in the standard hymnals. Where a hymn is used that is not widely known, a reference is usually made to a book in which it is included.

A page of notes, gathered from a variety of sources as I have met them in my reading, forms a general introduction to each chapter, to which it sustains a close relation. Another such page constitutes a general introduction to the entire volume. Occasionally a very brief hymn story is included in these pages. These notes will furnish speakers with good quotations.

WILLIAM J. HART.

Lacona, N. Y.

" Converse with one another in the music of psalms, in hymns, and in songs of the spiritual life, praise the Lord heartily with words and music, and render thanks to God the Father in the name of our Lord Jesus Christ at all times and for all things." (*Eph. 5: 19, 20. " A New Translation" by James Moffatt, D.D.*)

At a memorial service for Dr. Louis F. Benson, held in Philadelphia, Pa., on November 2, 1930, there was read this prayer which had been written by Dr. Benson, who was both a lover and a writer of hymns:

" We thank Thee, O God, for the long succession of Thy singers who have lifted Thy people's hearts and brightened their way with music; and we pray that we also may learn to greet the hard places of life with a song, and climbing steadfastly may enter into the fellowship of Thy white-robed choristers in heaven: through Jesus Christ our Lord. Amen."

" The Psalter still remains the noblest hymnal to be found in universal literature."—*Dean Howard Chandler Robbins.*

" The New Testament is the most radiant hymnbook ever written."—*Dr. John Paterson.*

" The literature of hymnology contains many masterpieces; innumerable hymns of the church are as beautiful in poetic art as they are devout in aspiration. If we took all the hymns out of English literature, the loss would be immeasurably huge."—*William Lyon Phelps.*

" The Bay Psalm Book was the first book printed in English in the United States (1640)—a Hymn Book! "—*Bulletin of The Hymn Society of America.*

CHAPTER I

STRANGE BUT TRUE

"There are times when everyone wants to sing."—*Elmer A. Leslie.*

> "I would be always in the thick of life,
> Threading its mazes, sharing in its strife,
> Yet—somehow, singing!

.   .   .   .

> "Not as one practiced in the singer's art,
> Nor always singing from a happy heart,
> But—somehow, singing!

.   .   .   .

> "When, at the road's end, shadows longer grow—
> Into the last long shadow let me go,
> Still—somehow, singing!"
> *—Roselle Mercier Montgomery*
> *in "The New York Times."*

"The world was born with music—when the 'stars first sang together.' The world was redeemed with music—'Peace on earth, good will toward men.' The world will end with music—'The song of Moses and the Lamb.' "—*The Rev. E. E. Helms, D.D.*

"Just as the preacher was about to start his sermon and had given out his text and theme on 'Christ and the Light of the World,' the church was suddenly plunged in complete darkness. There was an embarrassing silence when one of those on the platform started in a clear, strong voice:

> "'Let the lower lights be burning!
> Send a gleam across the wave!'

17

Instantly the great congregation was in song. Darkness was forgotten. A spiritual uplift had seized the embarrassed throng, and ere the chorus was closed, the lights came on.

" It was only a burned-out fuse, but night was transformed into day. Everyone was at ease; the preacher glowed in his message for a song had met a crisis and the Spirit of God spoke."—*John Timothy Stone, D.D.*

The Soloist in the Cell

Many of the prisoners were in solitary confinement, and hence a religious service for the inmates of Joliet Prison, Illinois, was held on this occasion in the corridors rather than in the chapel. Seated before the speaker, however, were eleven hundred people, some of whom were women.

A Presbyterian minister, the Rev. R. S. Snyder, D. D., was the speaker on that particular day. For many years Dr. Snyder has been (and still is, in 1940) the pastor of a large church in the city of Utica, New York. From him I received the story in detail. That day he did not talk on the parable of the Prodigal Son, as many do on such occasions. But he spoke on the theme (and text): " He made it again " (Jer. 18: 4). Toward the close of the address Dr. Snyder indicated what God had done through men and women who had been misguided, but who had later turned their steps toward Him.

The address closed, and the preacher was about to offer prayer. But " before I could begin to pray," said Dr. Snyder, " away down in the corridor of the women's section of the prison a sweet voice was heard in song." All were startled when they heard a woman, who, though unseen, was singing in her cell:

> " My faith looks up to Thee,
>   Thou Lamb of Calvary,
>   Saviour divine!
>   Now hear me while I pray,
>   Take all my guilt away,
>   O let me from this day
>   Be wholly Thine."

" It was more than a wonderful voice to me," added Dr. Snyder, " because the stone walls seemed to resound

as no opera ever would. I doubt whether in that great
company of men and women there was a dry eye. I found
myself unable to continue the service and pronounced the
benediction.

" Upon inquiry, I learned that the singer was a woman
with a splendid heritage and a musical background, who
somewhere along the road of life had missed the right
way. . . . Dr. MacDonald, who was then in charge of
the religious activities of Joliet Prison, has often referred
to this incident."

The singer, who was serving a life sentence, sang all
the stanzas of the hymn which voiced her penitence and
her prayer to Christ—" Take all my guilt away."

Through the corridors came the musical plea:

> " While life's dark maze I tread,
> And griefs around me spread,
>   Be Thou my guide;
> Bid darkness turn to day,
> Wipe sorrow's tears away,
> Nor let me ever stray
>   From Thee aside."

Thus did the repentant woman voice her desire that she
might henceforth be loyal to Christ.

Imprisoned for life! But penitence inspired hope.
Though she might never pass prison doors to freedom, yet
there was born a hope that she might pass from the prison
cell to the City of God. And so the woman sang the
prayer which doubtless expressed the desire of other
penitent prisoners who heard her song:

> " When ends life's transient dream,
> When death's cold, sullen stream
>   Shall o'er me roll;

Blest Saviour, then, in love,
Fear and distrust remove,
O bear me safe above,
A ransomed soul."

Though preacher, wardens and prisoners were startled by the song from the cell, yet the message in music lifted their thought beyond prison walls and gave them a glimpse of a forgiving Christ.

Author and Whistling Boy Met

" ' Are ye able,' said the Master,
  ' To be crucified with me? '—
' Yea,' the sturdy dreamers answered,
  ' To the death we follow Thee.'

" ' Lord we are able.
  Our spirits are Thine.
Remold them, make us,
  Like Thee, divine.
Thy guiding radiance
  Above us shall be
A beacon to God,
  To faith and loyalty.' " *

Whistling on his way home from the grocery store, a happy lad in a Missouri town was unaware that a professor from Boston University School of Theology (who later became its Dean) was listening to him. But it so happened that this stranger, motoring in the West on his way to Yellowstone Park, had some motor trouble. Therefore, while a mechanic was caring for the engine, the visitor walked down Main Street to make a few casual observations.

* This incident was supplied to the author by Doctor Marlatt; and both the story and the quotations from the hymn are used with his permission.

When he noticed the barefooted boy, he envied him the velvety dust between his toes; for the man himself was once a barefoot boy in a Midwestern town. Suddenly, however, he became interested in the tune the lad was whistling. It seemed to be like Harry Mason's music for the hymn " Challenge " which the visitor had written. Dr. Earl Marlatt (for it was he) listened intently. Was it really possible that this boy was whistling the tune of his hymn?

" No," he said to himself. " It couldn't be, away out here."

But he sauntered across the street, and spoke to the lad. " Hello, son," he said. " What's that you're whistling? "

His lips still pursed, the lad just naturally replied: " Oh, it's a song we sing at Sunday school: ' Are Ye Able? ' It's a honey. Did you ever hear it? "

" Listen, son," said the visitor, who confessed that he was " trying to be as clear-eyed " as the boy, " I wrote that song! "

" Think of that! " the little fellow exclaimed as he almost dropped his packages. " Do you mind if I tell the boys at Sunday school I saw you? "

" Not at all," Dean Marlatt assured the boy. Then he added: " That's the nicest compliment I ever got. Thank you very much."

" Aw, that's all right. Don't thank me. Thank you for writing the song. I won't forget. Good-bye."

The happy and surprised lad went down the street whistling:

> " ' Lord, we are able.
> Our spirits are Thine.' "

Mother Clark's Ebenezer Hymn

" Come, Thou Fount of every blessing,
　Tune my heart to sing Thy grace;
Streams of mercy, never ceasing,
　Call for songs of loudest praise.
Teach me some melodious sonnet
　Sung by flaming tongues above;
Praise the mount! I'm fixed upon it,
　Mount of Thy redeeming love."

Early in 1935 a New Year's article which I had written appeared in *Zion's Herald,* of Boston. In this article I had quoted four lines from the second stanza of Robert Robinson's hymn, " Come, Thou Fount," as follows:

" Here I raise mine Ebenezer;
　Hither by Thy help I'm come;
And I hope, by Thy good pleasure,
　Safely to arrive at home."

Within a few days after the publication of the article, a letter reached me from Mrs. Francis E. Clark, who, together with her husband, founded the Christian Endeavor Movement in Portland, Maine, February 2, 1881. So endeared did Dr. and Mrs. Clark become to young people of the Christian Endeavor societies that they later called them " Father " and " Mother " Clark.

Mrs. Clark, then, as she said, eighty-four years of age, wrote the letter in a firm, clear hand. After she had written an appreciative word concerning the article, she said: " I was especially pleased to note that you quoted a favorite verse of mine beginning:

" ' Here I raise mine Ebenezer.'

" Since you also like that verse, I thought you might be interested to know what it means to me. I was once humming that verse to myself, with a thankful heart for mercies past, when it suddenly occurred to me: But you have never raised your Ebenezer; Samuel put up a monument. Then I decided that I should really raise an Ebenezer of mine own, which should be a reminder of God's loving-kindness to me, as Samuel's monument was to the Israelites. (See I Samuel 7: 12.)

" At the first opportunity I went with my family to the beach, not far away (the letter was written from Newton, Massachusetts), and we each selected a stone that we liked and carried it home, and with these stones began to raise my Ebenezer. Not long after this, a little company of Christian Endeavorers called on me, and I suggested that they should each add a stone to my little monument, which they did, and we stood around the little monument and sang the hymn. In this way, from time to time, my own family and Christian Endeavor friends have added ' Stones of Help,' until it looks as you see it in this little snapshot elclosed."

" This hymn (written in 1758) for a hundred years has been a great favorite," said W. T. Stead. It now stands closely related to the religious life of Mrs. F. E. Clark, who did the uniquely beautiful thing of raising a mound of stones as a monument to her cherished song.

Heard Her Hymn When Living in Poorhouse

" When the mists have rolled in splendor
From the beauty of the hills,
And the sunlight falls in gladness
On the river and the rills,
We recall our Father's promise
In the rainbow of the spray:
We shall know each other better
When the mists have rolled away.

" We shall know as we are known,
Nevermore to walk alone,
In the dawning of the morning
Of that bright and happy day;
We shall know each other better,
When the mists have rolled away."

A girl of seventeen wrote a sacred song which was soon sung around the world, and which finally came back to her over the radio seventy years later when she was living in the poorhouse. The song written in her girlhood days brought back an encouraging and comforting message to the writer in her old age. Such was one of the strange experiences of life.

Born in Leon, New York, Annie Herbert died January 21, 1932, at the County Farm, three miles from San Rafael, California, at the age of eighty-eight. She became a school teacher at the period when the ministry of sacred song was becoming popular in evangelistic services. This young woman wrote several songs which were published, but she acquired fame through one—" When the Mists Have Rolled Away."

Having married a man named Barker, she and her husband moved to Montana, and were among the pioneers. In the year 1888 they made their residence in San Rafael, where they bought a home. Later the husband died, and the wife was left without an income. Unable to make needed repairs on the home, it eventually reached the condition where it did not afford sufficient protection. Mrs. Barker, therefore, on the advice of friends, moved to the County Farm, and there she spent the closing days of life.

Seeking confirmation of what seemed to be a strange story which was published in connection with the notice

of her death, a friendly local editor referred me to the
San Rafael Independent. Mr. Harry Lutgens, the editor and publisher, most kindly aided me by placing my
communication in the hands of Miss Florence G. Don-
nelly, a representative of the *Independent,* who was able
to supply me with many enlightening facts. Said she:

" I visited Mrs. Barker while she was at the Farm, and
although her mind was somewhat affected by her age, she
still was able to speak fluently; and she showed much evi-
dence of breeding and education. Friends who did not for-
sake her during her days of adversity arranged a fitting
funeral when she died. Mrs. Barker was an Episcopalian,
and the rector, the Rev. H. I. Oberholtzer, officiated at her
funeral services (January 23, 1932). A banker, Erwin
Holton, very appropriately rendered Mrs. Barker's own
song on that occasion."

The young lady who furnished me with these particu-
lars also confirmed the incident which was mentioned in
the first paragraph. A radio had been installed at the
County Farm for the purpose of providing entertainment
for the aged inmates. One evening a great surprise came
to Mrs. Barker and those who were with her when the
announcer stated that the next number would be devoted
to Annie Herbert (" wherever she may be "). Listening
intently, the aged lady, and those with her, were thrilled
when the soloist sang, " When the Mists Have Rolled
Away."

Aged, weak, dependent, there now came back to her
the message which she had given to the world when she
was but a girl. The shadows of life's eventide were gathering, and the woman who had gone through the days of
a long pilgrimage heard the lines which had comforted
countless thousands:

> " We shall come with joy and gladness,
>   We shall gather round the throne;
>   Face to face with those that love us
>   We shall know as we are known."

Long had the words of Annie Herbert Barker been carrying their songful message to other hearts, and now her hymn brought hope and joy to her own soul in her old age. For her the time was approaching

> " When we gather in the morning,
>   Where the mists have rolled away."

Baptismal Hymn for a Chinese General

> " O happy day, that fixed my choice
>   On Thee, my Saviour and my God!
>   Well may this glowing heart rejoice,
>   And tell its raptures all abroad."

The historic scene at Shanghai, China, when the head of the Chinese Republic, General Chiang Kai Shek, received the rite of Christian baptism, has been preserved for us by the Rev. J. C. Hawk, a missionary of the Methodist Church (at that time of the Methodist Episcopal Church, South). This was the report given in some American periodicals at the time:

" On October 23, 1930, at 3 o'clock, P. M., members of the immediate family and a few specially invited friends, Chinese and foreign, joined in this service at the home of Mrs. Chiang's mother, Mrs. K. T. Soong. . . . Dr. Z. T. Kaung, pastor of the Allen Memorial Church, Shanghai, was in charge of the ceremony.

" The services were held in the large reception room. . . . All sang together ' Happy Day.' Then the ritual ceremony of the Methodist Episcopal Church, South, for baptism and reception into the church was read by Dr. Kaung. Mr. Chiang stood by the side of General Chiang, and he . . . followed the service and answered quietly, but very clearly, each question as it was asked by the minister." The sacrament of the Lord's Supper was then administered.

Singularly strange and deeply impressive must it have been when that little company in China, on such a memorable occasion, united in singing

> " Happy day, happy day,
> When Jesus washed my sins away."

A Farmer's Hymn of the Holy Spirit

> " Holy Spirit, faithful Guide,
> Ever near the Christian's side;
> Gently lead us by the hand,
> Pilgrims in a desert land;
> Weary souls fore'er rejoice,
> While they hear that sweetest voice,
> Whispering softly, ' Wanderer, come!
> Follow me, I'll guide thee home.' "

Marcus Morris Wells was husking corn in his fields on a Saturday in October, 1858, when there came to him a suggestion for a hymn on the Holy Spirit. The next day, a stormy Sunday, he finished his hymn, and also composed a tune for the same—" Holy Spirit, Faithful Guide."

Two unusual facts are associated with this hymn and its author. The hymn has never been sung to any tune other than that which Mr. Wells composed; and, notwithstanding the popularity of this hymn, Mr. Wells wrote no others.

Mr. Wells, a descendant of Governor William Bradford, was born October 20, 1815, on a farm in the town of Otsego, in the State of New York. Most of his life, however, was spent in the little village of Hartwick, New York, where he engaged in farming; and where he also operated a small factory near his home. There he made small wooden farm tools. He was the inventor of a wooden barley-fork which had a wide sale.

Sundays he directed the choir in the village Baptist Church, and displayed a particular interest in sacred music. Mr. Sankey made frequent use of the hymn in religious meetings, and thus helped to make it popular. Soon it was translated into fifteen languages.

Mr. Wells died in Hartwick, July 17, 1895, and is buried four miles over the hills from the village. The opening line of his hymn is carved on his monument.

The first historical marker placed on Route 205, which passes the former home of Mr. Wells, by the State Bureau of Highways, was immediately in front of this house. This building was at that time the parsonage of the Congregational Church. The dedicatory service was held on the afternoon of Sunday, August 25, 1935. A large company of people assembled for the occasion. A nephew, George M. Augur, gave some personal memories of Mr. Wells. Clergymen of the village of Hartwick participated in the service. The entire company sang " Faith of Our Fathers " ; and the choir of the Baptist Church, among whom were some who sang forty years earlier with Mr. Wells, rendered:

" Holy Spirit, Faithful Guide."

The Baptist Church also has a unique memorial, which many people go to view. Facing the place where the preacher stands there is a wide art window. In its lower part there are inscribed the words of the hymn written by Mr. Wells:

HOLY SPIRIT, FAITHFUL GUIDE, EVER NEAR THE CHRISTIAN'S SIDE.

The words are also accompanied by notes of the tune composed by Mr. Wells.

On a day in mid-June, 1937, the writer accompanied a group of ministers from the city of Utica, and adjacent communities, who made a pilgrimage to Hartwick to view the scenes associated with the life of Mr. Wells. A resident of the community told us about the usefulness of this man of many activities, and mentioned his sterling character. Then we sang his hymn in the church where he himself sang.

Amid the peaceful scenes which he loved, the farmer and inventor lies at rest. But week after week, the year round, some congregations sing, as they assemble for worship, the hymn which he gave to the Christian world.

CHAPTER II

GREAT HYMNS ON HISTORIC OCCASIONS

" Jehovah is my strength and song." *(Psa. 118:14, R. V.)*

" Is ours a singing heart? Then it is a strong heart."—*Amos R. Wells.*

Historic Trinity Church, New York City, was filled with people who came from all over the great city, as the year 1930 came to a close, and 1931 dawned. A newspaper said, in describing the service: " At midnight the congregation joined in singing

" ' Nearer, my God, to Thee,'

as the chimes in the steeple pealed the same melody to hail the New Year."

Steeple bells and human voices thus blended in the venerable shrine of worship in one of the beloved hymns of the Christian Church as one year closed and another began.

" The occasion which led Luther to the writing of hymns is significant. In 1523 two youths were burnt to death, in the Grand Place at Brussels, for professing the reformed faith. They had died bravely singing the ' Te Deum.' . . . Their faithfulness filled Luther with joy."—" *The Evolution of the English Hymn,*" *by Frederick John Gilman, p. 131.*

" His (Theodore Roosevelt's) favorite hymn was ' How Firm a Foundation.' It alone was sung at his funeral. He could quote scores of hymns which he sang heartily. I saw him sing ' Ein' Feste Burg ' (Luther's battle hymn) in German with perfect ease without a book, with a group of delegates attending a Methodist General Conference."—*Dr. Christian F. Reisner in " The Christian Advocate."*

Psalm and Song After Fire

One of the great educational institutions for the training of women in the United States, Wellesley College, had a destructive fire on March 17, 1914. During the four hours the flames raged the administration offices were destroyed, as well as the recitation halls and the science laboratories. The college homes of three hundred and fifty students were burned, and most of the occupants lost their personal belongings. This fire, which leveled College Hall, made necessary the planning of a new Wellesley.

Though students lost their clothing in that early morning fire, yet, after a check was made, all were grateful that no life had been sacrificed. The students assembled for a chapel service soon after the fire had ceased its destructive work. President Ellen F. Pendleton was in charge, as faculty and students came together on this eventful morning for worship. Some were arrayed in bathrobes. President Pendleton must have prepared that service with the utmost care; and so she selected the passages of Scripture and the hymns which would comfort and soothe the frightened and nervous students who had passed through a harrowing experience. The assembled body read in unison the Ninety-first Psalm:

" He that dwelleth in the secret place of the most High shall abide under the shadow of the Almighty.
" I will say of the Lord, He is my refuge and my fortress: my God; in him will I trust."

The President followed by reading a selection from the New Testament, and then all rose to sing:

> "Who trusts in God, a strong abode
> In heaven and earth possesses;
> Who looks in love to Christ above,
> No fear his heart oppresses.
> In Thee alone, dear Lord, we own
> Sweet hope and consolation;
> Our shield from foes, our balm for woes,
> Our great and sure salvation."

The whole service, with appropriate Bible messages and a hymn of sustaining suggestion, must have made a deep impression. The faith of the President was magnificent in that hour. Though stating that college work would be immediately suspended, she yet announced that on April 7th it would be resumed. "The students," said a newspaper, "took a last look at the ashes, and then borrowed clothes in which to travel homeward."

Twenty years later, March 17, 1934, President Pendleton conducted a similar service for the undergraduates. The same Scriptures were read and the same hymn sung—"everything, except the emotional part, being the same as it was twenty years earlier." The students, many of whom were not born at the time of the fire, were greatly stirred by this commemoration, "yet they realized that a new and greater Wellesley had arisen from the ashes of the old building."

The hymn here mentioned is attributed by Dr. John Julian, the great authority, to Joachim Magdeburg. Therefore it dates back to the sixteenth century. Many hymnals do not include this selection, but it is found in "The Student Hymnary," edited by Dr. Edward Dwight Eaton. A translation into English was made by Benjamin H. Kennedy, a graduate of Cambridge University. "Jubilee" is the tune to which it is attached; and Dr. Eaton in his informing "Notes on the Hymns" (which are included in "The Student Hymnary") tells his readers that this tune, composed by Sir Arthur Sullivan, "was written for the Jubilee of Queen Victoria in 1897, to be sung with this hymn translated from the German."

Sung, therefore, by a mighty multitude on a day of a great national English celebration to express their gratitude for the reign of a beloved Queen, it was also used to voice the grateful feelings of a little group of shivering and nervous American college girls when fire destroyed both shelter and possessions.

Luther's Hymn in Luther's Land

Fourteen thousand Christian youth, from over forty nations and islands of the sea, assembled in monster mass meetings in Berlin in August, 1930. On a massive platform there was a chorus of over six hundred voices, and they were accompanied by an orchestra. The occasion was the Eighth World's Christian Endeavor Convention. Half a hundred meetings, as stated in the report of William Hiram Foulkes, Vice-President of the International Society of Christian Endeavor.

A memorable feature, the reports indicated, was the singing in a great hall by a crowded audience of Luther's tremendous song, "Ein' Feste Burg." The translation which Americans use is mostly the one given by Frederick H. Hedge:

> "A mighty fortress is our God,
>   A bulwark never failing;
> Our Helper He, amid the flood
>   Of mortal ills prevailing."

"Its majestic strains well-nigh rocked the sturdily steel-structured walls. Ambassador Sackett was present when Luther's mighty hymn was lifted as even an Ambassador had never heard it sung before."

The days of the convention ran swiftly to their close. "Then when the beloved leader of the whole Endeavor host, Dr. Daniel A. Poling, uttered the solemn words that dissolved the gathering amid the strains of Rankin's immortal hymn

"'God be with you till we meet again!'

with the tremendous Teutonic undertone 'Wiedersehen —Wiedersehen,' one felt stunned and overwhelmed— 'lost in wonder, love and praise.'"

When the young people of Christian Endeavor sang Luther's hymn they were singing what Dr. James Moffatt characterized as "the greatest hymn of the greatest man in the greatest period of German history." Luther not only wrote the hymn, but he also composed the tune to which it is invariably sung.

Writers of the history of hymns have given considerable space to the discussion of Luther's hymn. Dr. John Telford, an English authority, says: "The great chorale by Luther was published with the hymn in 1529. Words and music soon spread over Germany. It became the National Hymn and the battle-song of the nation. It was Luther's stay in some of the darkest hours of his life."

"Of English versions there have been many," said W. T. Stead. He added: "That of Thomas Carlyle is generally regarded as the best." This begins, as quoted by Stead:

" A sure stronghold our God is He.
A trusty shield and weapon;
Our help He'll be, and set us free
From every ill can happen."

Stead also quotes from Julian's "Dictionary of Hymnology" the German text:

" Ein' feste burg ist unser Gott."

Greatly have conditions changed in Germany since the youth of 1930 sang Luther's hymn in Luther's land. Luther not only wrote the hymn, but, by making some use of older sources, he also composed the tune to which it is invariably sung.

" Let goods and kindred go,
This mortal life also;
The body they may kill:
God's truth abideth still,
His kingdom is forever."

Hymn Brought Preachers to Their Feet

" When wilt Thou save the people?
O God of mercy, when?
The people, Lord, the people,
Not thrones and crowns, but men!
Flowers of Thy heart, O God, are they;
Let them not pass like weeds away,
Their heritage a sunless day.
God save the people! "

Though probably more used in England than in America, yet this hymn of Ebenezer Elliott, "The Sheffield Corn Law Rhymer," is sufficiently well known in the

United States to be included in "The Inter-Church Hymnal," as well as in "The Hymnal" (Episcopalian); "The Hymnal" (Presbyterian); "Hymns of the Spirit"; and "Hymns for Creative Living." It also finds a place in "The Hymnary" of the United Church of Canada. The Rev. Charles Garrett, a prominent English minister during the latter part of the last century, said: "This hymn rings in my mind like the cry of a nation on its knees." From a Scottish journalist comes this testimony: "So far as my experience goes, this hymn can raise great popular audiences as nothing else can. It seems to go right down to the hearts of the people, and it can be sung very effectively."

The author, born in 1781, died at Barnsley, 1849. He was in the habit of writing verses which appeared in a local newspaper. This hymn was published in a volume of his poems which appeared after his death. The author did not intend it to be used as a hymn; but after it was included in "The Congregational Church Hymnal," it was selected for other hymnals. The following interesting incident has been preserved by the Rev. John Telford, who says: "Elliott was led from a life of dissipation by seeing a primrose in Sowerby's '*Botany*,' and died with a wish on his lips to see it again." Elliott was "a forerunner of the social reformers of recent days." "Written to incite reforms of unhappy conditions in a particular era, the hymn is suitable to any age calling for movements for the betterment of the people."

Somewhere in the first decade of the present century the Rev. Dr. J. Ernest Rattenbury delivered an address at the Free Trade Hall, Manchester, England, in connection with the Free Church Council. "The subject was the implications and applications of the Gospel to the social

needs of mankind." That was a comparatively new subject in those days. He closed his address by quoting the
three stanzas of Elliott's poem,

> " When wilt Thou save the people?
> O God of mercy, when? "

Recalling the impassioned recital of that hymn, the
Rev. Walter H. Armstrong, who was present at the meeting, related this incident in an English periodical in
March, 1936. He said the speaker sat down. " But the audience rose up; staid and dignified preachers, not easily
moved, stood and waved their handkerchiefs or hats.
Rounds of deafening applause signified how greatly those
present were moved. Rarely, if ever, have I witnessed
such a triumph of passionate oratory. It was a great occasion, to be remembered as long as life shall last."

Mr. W. T. Stead speaks of this hymn as the " demo-
cratic anthem of the masses." And he also adds: " The
tune (Commonwealth) to which it is set, aptly fitted to
the words, has a great hold upon those who sing it."
What a heart-cry both sobs and sings itself in this hymn
with its social and humanitarian appeal! When one has
listened to the closing lines, whether read or sung, it is
difficult to forget them—

> " God save the people; Thine they are,
> Thy children, as Thine angels fair;
> From vice, oppression, and despair,
> God save the people! "

Salvation Army in Canterbury Cathedral

Historic Canterbury Cathedral added a new page to
its long and varied history near the close of November,

1931, when the Dean of Canterbury (Dr. Hewlett Johnson) extended an invitation to the Salvation Army to participate in a service in that renowned temple. Enthusiasm ran high, and a special train was chartered to convey members of the Salvation Army from different parts of Kent. Automobile loads of people "with happy, smiling faces, many framed in the familiar Hallelujah bonnet, brought life and color to the old Cathedral city." Said *The British Weekly,* in describing the scene: " The Salvation Army marched with bands playing and banners waving to the world-famed shrine of Thomas à Becket, where General Higgins, the Commander-in-Chief of the Salvation Army, preached the sermon at Evensong." . . .

" The large procession entered the Cathedral precincts in orderly rows with measured tread, the banners of a score of Salvation Army corps fluttering in the breeze. The Mayor and Corporation of Canterbury attended in state, and the massed bands led the singing with the Cathedral choir in attendance."

Three thousand people crowded into the nave of the Cathedral, and many others were unable to gain admission. " The musical part of the service left nothing to be desired, and the mellow notes of the grand organ blended delightfully with the sonorous brass of the Army bands. The historic service concluded with Isaac Watts' hymn, ' Jesus Shall Reign,' which was sung to the tune of ' Rimington.' "

Eminently fitting was it that this great meeting should thus close. The Salvation Army has carried its flag, indicative of spiritual conquest, over the world. Appropriately, therefore, when it was accorded such exceptional recognition, did its bands lead in singing this hymn of one of the greatest hymn writers of the Christian Church, which has been characterized as " the first confident missionary pronouncement in modern hymnody." The notes of grandeur, triumph and prophecy are found in the appealing lines of this " greatest of all missionary hymns, a rendering of Psalm 72 into Christian song," by Isaac Watts:

" Jesus shall reign where'er the sun
Does his successive journeys run;
His kingdom spread from shore to shore,
Till moons shall wax and wane no more.

" To Him shall endless prayer be made,
And endless praises crown His head;
His name, like sweet perfume, shall rise
With every morning sacrifice."

Canon Sheppard Led in Wesley's Hymn

Four thousand men and women crowded into historic St. Paul's Cathedral, London, for the Diamond Jubilee Thanksgiving Service of the National Brotherhood and Sisterhood movements in March, 1936. This meeting was held after the regular evening service in the Cathedral, and the members of the congregation had come from various counties. Canon H. R. L. Sheppard, who was in charge of the service, expressed the hope that all would feel as much at home as though they were in their own places of worship; and the visitors were urged " not to allow the dignity and beauty of the Cathedral to lessen their fervor."

The hymn selected to open the service was Charles Wesley's—

" O for a thousand tongues to sing
My great Redeemer's praise,
The glories of my God and King,
The triumphs of His grace."

Canon Sheppard himself led the singing. A visitor made the observation that " it was good to see an Anglican Canon in a Cathedral waving his arms to inspire the singing of Wesley's hymn."

London newspapers spoke of the happy fellowship of that group of men and women, who rejoiced in a Christian experience. From different denominations they came; yet in majestic St. Paul's they united happily in singing:

" Jesus! the name that charms our fears,
That bids our sorrows cease,
'Tis music in the sinner's ears,
'Tis life, and health, and peace."

Charles Wesley wrote this hymn in 1739 to celebrate the first anniversary of his spiritual birth. But, as W. T. Stead says in " Hymns That Have Helped," " The first man that this hymn helped was Charles Wesley himself." Most assuredly, however, it has also helped many thousands since; and among lovers of hymns it continues to be a great favorite.

Hymn Loved by Both King and Poet

New associations cluster around one of our best known and most cherished hymns because it became linked with both the famous writer, Rudyard Kipling, and also England's beloved King, George V, in January, 1936, and was sung at the funeral of each.

When Kipling was buried in Westminster Abbey, January 23rd, and shown the highest distinction which the British Empire could give him at his death, there naturally was sung his own "Recessional." Through the ancient temple, where lie the honored sons of the nation, there sounded the majestic strains—

> "God of our fathers, known of old,
> Lord of our far-flung battle line,
> Beneath whose awful hand we hold
> Dominion over palm and pine:
> Lord God of Hosts, be with us yet,
> Lest we forget, lest we forget!"

Very different was the other musical selection, which the Associated Press said was "Kipling's favorite hymn":

> "Abide with me: fast falls the eventide;
> The darkness deepens; Lord, with me abide!
> When other helpers fail, and comforts flee,
> Help of the helpless, O abide with me."

Just five days later, January 28th, 1936, King George V was laid to rest with his fathers at Windsor. Again the hymn of Henry F. Lyte was sung:

> "Abide with me: fast falls the eventide.
>
> .   .   .   .
>
> "Hold Thou Thy cross before my closing eyes;
> Shine through the gloom and point me to the skies;
> Heaven's morning breaks, and earth's vain shadows flee;
> In life, in death, O Lord, abide with me."

"This was King George's favorite hymn which the monarch sang in the little parish church at Sandringham on Christmas Day, the last service King George attended in life," we were told by the Associated Press.

Immediately following the line

" In life, in death, O Lord, abide with me,"

the Archbishop of Canterbury, who a few days before had stood by the bedside of the dying monarch at Sandringham, read the committal service.

The newspapers reported that at football games held in England on the Saturday previous to the funeral (January 25th) the large groups assembled reverently stood and sang, " Abide with Me," in memory of the beloved King. Sunday, the land over, as well as in some other countries, this was one of the hymns sung by congregations at their services of worship. Thus a great hymn, which stood second in a list of a " Hundred Best Hymns " selected in 1887, won an even warmer place in the hearts of the people. Having been sung at the funeral of both a King and a poet of fame in less than a week, this hymn was shown to have a firm hold on the hearts of Christian men and women everywhere; and the song became a prayer.

Hymn Heard " From Coast to Coast "

For the first time the National Sunday Forum became a part of the life of the entire American nation on the afternoon of the first Sunday in 1932. The music of the singers assembled in the studio in New York City and the address of Dr. S. Parkes Cadman were that day heralded " from coast to coast." Therefore it was an event of significance in the life of the nation. I happened to be among those listening to the program. What hymns, one wondered, would be selected to inaugurate this new feature? The New Year found the people in the midst of anxiety, unemployment and depression. What, therefore, would be the first musical message to the homes of the American people in such an eventful period? The question was answered in a most delightful manner when the musicians began the words of that hymn which has so firmly gripped the life of the Christian Church in the twentieth century:

> " Where cross the crowded ways of life,
>   Where sound the cries of race and clan,
>   Above the noise of selfish strife,
>   We hear Thy voice, O Son of Man! "

Though this hymn belongs to the first decade of our own century, yet it has become so rapidly popular that in 1930 the "Inter-Church Hymnal" listed it as number 61 among the hymns used in Sunday worship in the United States. It has also gone overseas, and is found in British hymnals. In fact, Dr. Robert Guy McCutchan says, " Probably no other hymn in recent years has been included in so many different types of books of sacred song."

At the time the hymn was written (in 1903), Dr. Frank Mason North was the Corresponding Secretary of the New York City Missionary and Church Extension Society, connected with the Methodist Episcopal Church. Therefore he knew the life of the city and the needs of its people. " This is a city mission hymn in the best sense." Said the Rev. John Telford, B.A., who was one of the foremost authorities on hymnology in England: " Verse 5 is a plaintive cry for the Master's presence and help, and verse 6 sees the glorious city descending out of heaven." These are the two verses thus mentioned:

" O Master, from the mountain side,
 Make haste to heal these hearts of pain;
 Among these restless throngs abide,
 O tread the city's streets again.

" Till sons of men shall learn Thy love
 And follow where Thy feet have trod;
 Till glorious from Thy heaven above
 Shall come the city of our God! "

Whoever selected the hymn for that January Sunday, when its strains were destined to be heard " from coast to coast," made a wisely appropriate choice.

Dedicatory Hymns at Radio City

The dedicatory services of the Radio Pulpit, in connection with Radio City, New York City, were conducted on Sunday, November 12, 1933. The speakers of the occasion were Dr. S. Parkes Cadman, minister of the Radio Pulpit; Dr. Ralph W. Sockman, who became Dr. Cadman's successor in this service; and Dr. Frederick K. Stamm. Following very brief addresses by these prominent clergymen, some hymns were sung. I happened to be listening to this service in my home, two hundred miles from New York City. " What hymns will be used for such a significant occasion as this? " I asked myself. Soon came the answer. Three hymns were announced, and two stanzas of each were rendered. They came in the following order:

" O worship the King, all-glorious above,
O gratefully sing His power and His love;
Our Shield and Defender, the Ancient of Days,
Pavilioned in splendor, and girded with praise.

" O tell of His might, O sing of His grace,
Whose robe is the light, whose canopy space;
His chariots of wrath the deep thunder-clouds form,
And dark is His path on the wings of the storm."

This devotional hymn of adoration was a beautiful recognition of the majestic King of the universe. The next hymn that was sung told of the exaltation of Christ, and is prophetic of His peaceful conquests:

" Hail, to the Lord's Anointed,
    Great David's greater Son!
Hail, in the time appointed,
    His reign on earth begun!
He comes to break oppression,
    To set the captive free;
To take away transgression,
    And rule in equity.

.   .   .   .   .   .

" He shall come down like showers
    Upon the fruitful earth,
Love, joy and hope, like flowers,
    Spring in His path to birth:
Before Him on the mountains,
    Shall peace, the herald, go,
And righteousness, in fountains,
    From hill to valley flow."

The closing hymn was a petition for Divine leadership, and an expression of readiness to follow in the direction led:

" Lead on, O King Eternal,
   The day of march has come;
Henceforth in fields of conquest
   Thy tents shall be our home:
Through days of preparation
   Thy grace has made us strong,
And now, O King Eternal,
   We lift our battle song."

The occasion was Armistice Sunday, therefore it was beautifully appropriate that the last verse sung that day should be

" Lead on, O King Eternal,
   Till sin's fierce war shall cease,
And Holiness shall whisper
   The sweet Amen of peace;
For not with swords loud clashing,
   Nor roll of stirring drums;
With deeds of love and mercy,
   The heavenly kingdom comes."

Introduced by these great hymns, the new Radio Pulpit entered on its welcome and far-reaching ministry. Through its agency those isolated by distance and winter storm receive the gospel message; and the many confined to the home by age and illness can listen to the service of song, sermon and prayer.

A Pilgrimage of Hymn Lovers

" Rock of Ages, cleft for me,
   Let me hide myself in Thee;
Let the water and the blood,
   From Thy wounded side which flowed,
Be of sin the double cure,
   Save from wrath and make me pure."

"No other English hymn can be named which has laid so firm and broad a grasp upon the English-speaking world," wrote Dr. John Julian in his "Dictionary of Hymnology," when discussing the universally known hymn of Toplady's "Rock of Ages." Nutter and Tillett made this comment: "To write a hymn so popular and so useful is a privilege an angel might covet." When, early in 1887, the editors of *The Sunday at Home* invited their readers to send lists of the Hundred English Hymns which stood highest in their esteem, nearly thirty-five hundred persons responded. "Rock of Ages" headed the list with 3,215 votes.

This hymn dates back to 1776, at which time the author was thirty-six years of age. The occasion on which Toplady received the inspiration for his immortal hymn has been indicated by the Rev. John Telford in "The New Methodist Hymn Book Illustrated," * where he says: "Sir William Henry Wills, in a letter to Dean Lefroy, published in the *Times* in June, 1898, says, 'Toplady was one day overtaken by a thunderstorm in Burrington Combe, on the edge of my property, Blagdon (where he was then curate), a rocky glen running up into the heart of the Mendip range, and there, taking shelter between two massive piers of our native limestone rock, he penned the hymn:

> "'Rock of Ages, cleft for me,
> Let me hide myself in Thee.'

There is a precipitous crag of limestone a hundred feet high, and right down its center is the deep recess in which Toplady sheltered."

* Published by The Epworth Press, London, 1934.

The privilege of joining with others in singing a famous hymn amid the surroundings by which it was inspired is one rarely enjoyed. Imagine, therefore, the joy of thirty thousand people when they assembled on a day in late summer, in 1935, in Somerset, at the very place where Toplady is assumed to have received the suggestion for his immortal hymn. This happened when a daily newspaper in Bristol organized the pilgrimage which took the many thousands of people to the historic site. It was a tremendous success. In fact, the following day the same newspaper called it "Modern England's Greatest Pilgrimage of Devotion."

An account of this eventful day appeared in *The Methodist Recorder*, London (August 8, 1935), from the pen of the Rev. R. R. Tregunna, in which he indicated that for long years many had cherished the desire "to visit the sacred spot, and to climb into the great cleft rock for themselves, surrounded by the lofty grandeur of the Mendips, and to join in singing in its birthplace the hymn that has brought comfort to innumerable men and women. The noble setting of the vast natural amphitheater (at Burrington Combe, Somerset), with hundreds of young people in eerie places high up on the hillside, and some of them looking no bigger than birds, seemed only to increase the awe and solemnity of the scene."

The great crowd, which included a large proportion of young people, was naturally in a singing mood. First they sang:

"All people that on earth do dwell."

Then came:

"Guide me, O Thou great Jehovah: "

and the leader, F. A. Wiltshire, made the statement that
this hymn by William Williams was first published in
Wine Street, Bristol, "the street where Whitefield welcomed John Wesley to Bristol."

The masterpiece of Charles Wesley could not be
omitted on such a jubilant occasion, and so they sang:

> "Jesus, Lover of my soul,
>   Let me to Thy bosom fly."

The people who sang joyfully also gave liberally. Following an appeal by the Lord Mayor, an offering of
ninety-seven pounds was received for the hospitals of
Bristol.

An address was made by Dean Blackburne in which
he stated that the hymn of Toplady made a universal appeal because "it expressed the universal need of the soul
for stability in a world of change." The great moment
for which the people had been waiting then came, and
the thirty thousand people blended their voices in the
familiar lines:

> "Rock of Ages, cleft for me,
>   Let me hide myself in Thee."

"The people evidently came to sing," said Mr. Tregunna. "There was a depth of conviction in the singing
by these thousands that was deeply impressive. The hymn
was sung a second time to another tune, and again the
people let themselves go." What a thrilling and memorable moment!

King, Queen and Farmers Sang Together in Canada

" I to the hills will lift mine eyes;
    From whence doth come mine aid?
My safety cometh from the Lord,
    Who heaven and earth hath made.

" Thy foot He'll not let slide, nor will
    He slumber that thee keeps.
Behold, He that keeps Israel
    He slumbers not, nor sleeps."

King George and Queen Elizabeth worshipped on Sunday, June 4, 1939, while making the historic trip to Canada, and later to the United States, in the United Church at Portage La Prairie, " in the heart of Manitoba's wheat belt." Said the Canadian Press: " In the quiet of the large stone church the King and Queen expressed their thanks to the minister. Her Majesty described it as ' an oasis,' after a crowded week which took them to the Pacific Coast and back to the prairies."

The minister who conducted the service was the Rev. George W. Abernathy. He was described as " a ' Dundee lad,' who came to Canada twenty years ago to labor in the mission fields of Northern Saskatchewan." He afterward said that Her Majesty was interested to learn, as she talked with him at the close of the service (as did also the King) that he was born in Angus County, Scotland, " her own county."

The hymn which opened the service was from the Scottish Psalter, and dates back to 1650. It is included among the " Psalms in Metre " which appear in " The Hymnary " of the United Church of Canada. Said the Canadian Press, in describing the service:

" Both the King and Queen joined with the fifty-voice choir under the leadership of choirmaster-organist James D. McRae, in the singing of the hymns—' I to the Hills Will Lift Mine Eyes,' an ancient Scottish song, and another old favorite, ' My Faith Looks Up to Thee.' The anthem was ' God is a Spirit,' by Bennett, sung by the choir." The heading given to this item in the Canadian Press was " Royalty Worship with Farm People." Thus King, Queen and farmers sang together one of the " Songs of Zion."

Song Sung by Uniting Churches

" The Church's one foundation
    Is Jesus Christ her Lord.

.   .   .   .   .   .

" Elect from every nation,
    Yet one o'er all the earth,
Her charter of salvation,
    One Lord, one faith, one birth;
One holy Name she blesses,
    Partakes one holy food,
And to one hope she presses,
    With every grace endued."

Methodists from many lands assembled in Grace and Holy Trinity Cathedral, Kansas City, Missouri, on the morning of April 26, 1939, for holy communion. This gathering was one of the most historic assemblies ever held by a religious organization in the United States. Representatives of the Methodist Episcopal Church, the Methodist Episcopal Church, South, and the Methodist

Protestant Church, long divided by conflicting opinions, were about to re-unite in one great family of almost eight million members. And this company who were " bowing in reverent silence amid the rugged stone beauty of an Episcopal Church" consisted of the nine hundred delegates who were on that day assembled for the Uniting Conference which overcame the divisions of the past, and once more made them one. The oldest delegate was eighty-eight; but there were some not far advanced in their twenties. That day those men and women were both dreaming dreams and seeing visions, as they observed the sacrament of the Lord's Supper.

Led by a company of youthful trumpeters and the Boston University Seminary Singers the bishops and the nine hundred delegates marched, two by two, the two blocks which took them to the Municipal Auditorium, where the Uniting Conference was to be held. The company sang as they went. Many people witnessed the great processional. The last strains of music at the cathedral were:

> " Lead on, O King Eternal:
> We follow, not with fears,
> For gladness breaks like morning
> Where'er Thy face appears."

The first words as they reached the Auditorium were:

> " All hail the power of Jesus' Name!
> Let angels prostrate fall;
> Bring forth the royal diadem,
> And crown Him Lord of all."

Soon the delegates were seated, and all around them in the immense building were visitors assembled to witness the proceedings of the memorable gathering. The first hymn announced, having been carefully selected in advance, was one eminently fitting for such a day as this:

> " The Church's one foundation
>   Is Jesus Christ her Lord;
> She is His new creation
>   By water and the word:
> From heaven He came and sought her
>   To be His holy bride;
> With His own blood He bought her,
>   And for her life He died."

Wednesday evening, May 10, 1939, there came " The Declaration of Union," and the three bodies mentioned became The Methodist Church. " A hushed assemblage of more than twelve thousand people crowded every available seat of the Auditorium " for the significant occasion. That service began, like the first, with the hymn, " The Church's One Foundation." When the Declaration of Union was declared adopted " The Hallelujah Chorus " from Handel's " Messiah " was rendered by the Greater Kansas City Messiah Chorus.

Just before the final benediction of the last session that vast company most feelingly sang the undying hymn of Isaac Watts:

> " O God, our help in ages past,
>   Our hope for years to come."

Significant is the fact that the same hymn was chosen to open both the first and the last sessions of the Uniting Conference of American Methodism. Yet, undoubtedly, it was the most appropriate which could have been selected. It was written by the Rev. Samuel J. Stone, an

English clergyman, when the author was twenty-seven years of age, and is one that people love to sing. It has become one of the great processionals of the Christian Church, and that foremost authority, Dr. John Julian, termed it a " magnificent hymn."

Most writers on hymnology relate the fact that this hymn was chosen for one of the great historic gatherings of Christendom. Hence " during the Lambeth Conference of 1888 each of three imposing services, at Canterbury Cathedral, Westminster Abbey, and St. Paul's Cathedral, was opened by the words and music of this hymn, as leaders from every part of the ecclesiastical world moved through the stately aisles." The effect at St. Paul's on this occasion was almost overwhelming. Impressed with the majestic strains of this hymn, Bishop Nelson, of New Zealand, paid tribute to the same at the close of the Lambeth Conference in these graceful lines:

> " Bard of the Church, in these divided days
> For words of harmony to thee be praise:
> Of love and oneness thou dost strike the chords,
> And set our thoughts and prayers to tuneful words.
>
> . . . . . .
>
> From Lambeth towers to far New Zealand's coast,
> Bard of the Church, thy blast inspires the host."

When the American Nation Sang Matheson's Hymn

Mrs. Calvin Coolidge went out to do her morning shopping on January 5, 1933, at Northampton, Massachusetts, and when she returned she found her distinguished husband dead. Death had come with swift suddenness to the man who less than four years before had retired from the presidency of the United States.

The following Saturday, January 7th, the former President was buried, and the funeral services were held at the Edwards Congregational Church, in Northampton, where the family were accustomed to worship.

Newman's "Lead, Kindly Light" was sung at the opening of the service; but the hymn which came later was one which Mrs. Coolidge particularly requested. This, she indicated, was the favorite of Mr. Coolidge. Therefore the greatly beloved hymn, written by Scotland's blind preacher, Dr. George Matheson, was rendered that day by a quartette—

> " O Love that wilt not let me go,
>   I rest my weary soul in Thee;
> I give Thee back the life I owe,
> That in Thine ocean depths its flow
>   May richer, fuller be."

With her son John by her side, the woman who had lost her other son, Calvin, Jr., while the family occupied the White House, listened to the voices which sang those words of challenge, resignation and hope:

> " O Cross that liftest up my head,
>   I dare not ask to fly from Thee;
> I lay in dust life's glory dead,
> And from the ground there blossoms red
>   Life that shall endless be."

Three visiting ministers conducted a service of worship in the little community church in Plymouth, Vermont, the next day. This was the birthplace of Mr. Coolidge, and there, in the cemetery by the roadside, near the home of his boyhood, his body had been laid to rest after being taken from Northampton at the close of the service in the historic church. Neighbors of the Coolidge family, who had known "Calvin" all his life, came together in sorrow, and yet in pride, that day. The body of the ex-President was now resting in their own cemetery. The man, who had visited his mother's grave to pray when he assumed the presidency in a unique manner, had achieved distinction and rendered most valuable national service. Now amid the scenes of his youth he was reposing in "God's Acre."

The family pew was that day unoccupied in the sanctuary at Plymouth. Draped in black, it was marked by an American flag. But the little congregation, with tender memories of the man they loved and with tear-filled eyes, sang:

"O Love that wilt not let me go."

That Sunday almost every congregation in America also heard the former President's favorite hymn during the day. One editor suggested that probably on just one other occasion did so many American congregations sing the same hymn, and that was on the Sunday following the death of President William McKinley, when his cherished hymn, "Nearer, My God, to Thee," was almost universally rendered by the churches of the land.

Radio, however, had come into general use since the death of President McKinley. So, on Sunday, January 8, 1933, Dr. S. Parkes Cadman, whose voice was heard "from coast to coast," uttered words of tribute to the memory of Mr. Coolidge, and then asked his invisible audience all over the country to rise while the choir in the studio rendered the hymn which had acquired even deeper significance because of its association with the man the nation honored and loved. Hence in places far

distant from New York City people reverently stood by
the side of their radios and listened to Matheson's immortal and soul-reaching song:

> " O love that wilt not let me go,
> I rest my weary soul in Thee."

A Queen's Selection of Hymns

> " Our blest Redeemer, ere He breathed
> His tender last farewell,
> A Guide, a Comforter, bequeathed
> With us to dwell.

> .   .   .   .   .   .

> " He comes sweet influence to impart,
> A gracious, willing Guest
> While He can find one humble heart
> Wherein to rest."

Fog delayed the arrival of King George VI and Queen
Elizabeth when they made their historic visit to Canada
and the United States in the early summer of 1939. Hence
the Canadian Press said in an item dated May 14, " The
liner *Empress of Australia* (carrying these royal person-
ages) came in sight of land today." This was on Sunday.
The item added that the liner " had been scheduled to
dock at Quebec today, and now is due to land her royal
passengers Wednesday morning."

Then was added this information: " Divine service,
the second observed aboard since the liner sailed from
Portsmouth, England, May 6, was conducted during the
morning with Purser D. F. Armour reading the lesson."
Hymns for the service, it was mentioned, were selected
by Queen Elizabeth.

The Queen, we were told, made the following selections:

> " All people that on earth do dwell,
>   Sing to the Lord with cheerful voice."

This hymn (from the 100th Psalm) made a praiseful opening for the service of worship.

The second hymn was—

> " Hark, my soul! it is the Lord.
>   'Tis thy Saviour, hear His word."

William Cowper, who " gave expression to real human emotion," was the author of this song, which was included in the " Olney Hymns."

Ascension Day was observed the Thursday before, so this was the first Sunday after Ascension. Doubtless, therefore, this fact was in the mind of Queen Elizabeth, and guided her in the choice of the third hymn:

> " Our blest Redeemer, ere He breathed
>   His tender last farewell."

This hymn, first published in 1829, came into common use slowly; but when compilers of hymnals came to recognize its great merit the hymn attained wide popularity. It is now popularly ranked among the chief hymns concerning the Holy Spirit. Most modern hymnals include these verses, and Covert and Laufer indicate that " it is decidedly popular in American churches."

Harriet Auber, who wrote the hymn, was born in London, October 4, 1773, and lived until January 20, 1862. Her father was a clergyman in the Church of England. John B. Dykes composed the tune " St. Cuthbert " for these words. Thus the hymn of a lady who spent most of the eighty-nine years of her life " in cultured seclusion " in quiet English villages made in this hymn (as well as in others) a most valuable addition to the songs of the Christian Church, and a hundred and ten years after its composition a British Queen selected her hymn as one to be sung when making a memorable voyage. Together, crew and passengers sang as the service was drawing to a close on the Ascension Sunday:

> " Spirit of purity and grace,
>   Our weakness, pitying, see;
>   O make our hearts Thy dwelling place,
>   And worthier Thee! "

CHAPTER III

MUSIC AND MEMORY

"I find myself still humming the old hymns and tunes."—
Miss Ellen Wilkinson, M.P.

"Wondrous power of music! It touches the chords of memory, and brings back the happy scenes of the past.

"In the rude mining camp, cut off by the snows of winter, in the narrow cabin of the ship ice-bound in the Arctic seas, in the bare, dark rooms of the war-prison where the captive soldiers are trying to beguile the heavy time in company, tears steal down the rough cheeks when someone strikes up the familiar notes of 'Home, Sweet Home.'"—*Henry van Dyke.*

"I can never come upon that beautiful prayer

"'Father, whate'er of earthly bliss,'

without seeing our room with all the family gathered together and singing together. For that was one of the few hymns we sang every Sunday evening. I recall how the first gospel hymns caught us and excited us. I remember vividly the first time we came upon the hymn,

"'Holy, holy, holy! Lord God Almighty!'

to Dyke's tune. I can still feel the thrill of joy its beauty roused. I remember the first time I ever heard

"'Now the day is over,'

to Barnby's setting. It seemed as if heaven itself could hold nothing more lovely."—*William P. Merrill, D.D.*, in a sermon delivered at the service held in memory of Dr. Louis F. Benson, D.D., under the auspices of the Hymn Society of America.

What the Artist Heard and Believed

A boy stood up behind a big gas burner during a cottage prayer meeting in a New England community, and said, "I want to be a Christian." The timid lad made this confession with fear and trembling.

A few years later, having reached manhood, he was talking over some problems with a good deacon. Said the latter to him: "Do you remember the tune Ellen Gannett started the night you stood up back of the stove?" The young man did. "Nobody who ever sang that from the heart ever got lost in this world or the next," affirmed the deacon.

Henry Turner Bailey, who later became a renowned teacher of art, was the boy. The song sung by the little group in the prayer meeting was:

> "I am Thine, O Lord, I have heard Thy voice,
>   And it told Thy love to me;
> But I long to rise in the arms of faith,
>   And be closer drawn to Thee."

The refrain is familiar at devotional services:

> "Draw me nearer, nearer, blessed Lord,
>   To the cross where Thou hast died;
> Draw me nearer, nearer, nearer, blessed Lord,
>   To Thy precious, bleeding side."

Forty years later Mr. Bailey related the incident, and gave this written testimony: "Since then I have never had a doubt of the love of God or of His readiness to guide one who is willing to be guided."

Mr. Ira D. Sankey has told us that during his singing

days this hymn was extensively used by the societies of Christian Endeavor both in the United States and Great Britain. Also, he has informed us ("My Life and the Story of the Gospel Hymns") how the words and the music came directly from the hearts of author and composer:

"Fanny Crosby was visiting Mr. W. H. Doane in his home in Cincinnati, Ohio. They were talking about the nearness of God, as the sun was setting and the evening shadows were gathering around them. The subject so impressed the well-known hymn writer, that before retiring she had written the words to this hymn, which has become one of the most useful she has ever written. The music by Mr. Doane so well fitted the words that the hymn has become a special favorite wherever the Gospel Hymns are known."

Father and Son Sang Together

An elderly man, whose name was not given, wrote to *The British Weekly* saying, "I wonder whether other readers share my experience in which the singing of certain hymns conjures up a vivid scene from the past? . . . I mean that by the singing of these hymns I seem to be actually transported to other scenes."

Three hymns were mentioned by him, as recalling these great memories in his hymn-singing life. The second of the three was—

> "Thou Shepherd of Israel, and mine,
> The joy and desire of my heart,
> For closer communion I pine,
> I long to reside where Thou art:

> The pasture I languish to find
>   Where all, who their Shepherd obey,
> Are fed, on Thy bosom reclined,
>   And screened from the heat of the day."

" It is the last night of my son's last leave before he goes to his ship in 1915, never to return—though we didn't know that. We sing the hymn round the piano. Today I try to recall that boy's voice; I can't, even his features are hazy, *until that hymn is sung;* then I hear the actual tones of his voice and see his face as though he stood beside me. As the hymn ends I lose him again." Thus wrote the father in his letter, as he associated music and memory.

This hymn by Charles Wesley does not hold a place in American hymnals, but it is found in " The Methodist Hymn Book," published in London in 1933, where it is joined with the tune " Arabia."

When Floating in the Atlantic

Hymns link themselves with life in strange ways and at unexpected times. A story published by C. Harold Lowden in *The Christian Advocate* (January 14, 1937) confirms this statement. Mr. Lowden composed the tune " Living for Jesus " to accompany the song written by T. O. Chisholm—

> " Living for Jesus a life that is true,
>   Striving to please Him in all that I do,
> Yielding allegiance, glad-hearted and free,
>   This is the pathway of blessing for me."

The incident related by Mr. Lowden concerns itself with Miss Emily C. Beck, a member of the Christian Endeavor Society of Trinity Reformed Church, Philadelphia, Pennsylvania. Several years earlier she had become acquainted with the song and its tune; and she and her sister committed to memory the four stanzas and the chorus.

Meantime Miss Beck had become the secretary of a prominent physician in Philadelphia. Having been advised to take a complete rest during her vacation, she engaged passage for a trip to Cuba. After an enjoyable voyage and a delightful experience in Cuba, she was returning home. All the associations were pleasant, and the weather was perfect. Then, just off the coast of New Jersey, there came intimations that all was not well with the ship. " Later the order was heard, ' Don the life-belts.' Finally, ' Jump into the sea.' Horror-stricken, Miss Beck obeyed the order. Soon she was floundering in the open sea, so terrorized that she could do nothing but float." This young woman had been a passenger on the *Morro Castle,* which caught fire off Asbury Park, and was almost completely destroyed.

Suddenly there came to her mind the hymn that she had memorized ten years earlier. Soon she was singing " Living for Jesus." The entire hymn was sung. Cold and numb, and near to losing consciousness repeatedly, she, again and again, raised her voice in song until she heard reassuring words from a rescuing party, then she lapsed into unconsciousness.

This story was later told by Miss Beck " with grateful joy to thousands of young people." Naturally, they have been deeply thrilled as they have heard her relate how the hymn sustained her that night while adrift on the broad Atlantic with no help in sight. From the treasure house of memory there came a Christian song, learned in early life, which brought courage, trust and hope in time of need.

Judge Quoted Hymn to Lad

" Something novel in reform was introduced into Harlem Court today by Magistrate Benjamin Greenspan," reported the United Press on a summer day in 1932. A youth, named Prince, was before him, charged with vagrancy. The boy was only nineteen, and evidently the heart of the judge was sympathetic toward the lad.

The novel feature consisted in the fact that the judge quoted some lines from an old gospel song, as follows:

> " Down in the human heart
> Crushed by the tempter,
> Feelings lie buried that grace can restore;
> Touched by a loving heart,
> Wakened by kindness,
> Chords that were broken will vibrate once more."

" Prince, standing attentive, wept when the judge had finished; and there was scarcely a dry eye in the courtroom," commented the newspaper item. The quotation of the song had accomplished its purpose.

Sentence was suspended. The young man made a note of the verse, and held the copy in his hand as he left the room. The judge, however, could not recall the author. Evidently it was a memory from his early days in the Sunday school, or from some church services, for the stanza came from one of the best known gospel songs of Fanny J. Crosby, America's blind singer. Multitudes have been strangely touched as they have united in singing:

> " Rescue the perishing,
> Care for the dying,
> Snatch them in pity from sin and the grave;

Weep o'er the erring one,
Lift up the fallen,
Tell them of Jesus the mighty to save.

"Rescue the perishing,
Care for the dying;
Jesus is merciful,
Jesus will save."

Hymns are heard in unexpected places (even in the halls of justice), and their words long ring in the heart. When the singer is forgotten, the song is remembered.

Archbishop's Memory of a Hymn

The Archbishop of Canterbury delivered the sermon at the Wesley Bicentenary Evensong at St. Paul's Cathedral, London, May 25, 1938. At that time the Archbishop related this incident:

"I cannot but recall an experience of my own, for I think John Wesley would understand it. I was once about to speak to a great crowd of working men in the North of England on social questions. As I went to my place they were singing, as only North-countrymen can sing:

"'Tell me the story softly,
With earnest tones and grave;
Remember, I'm the sinner
Whom Jesus came to save.'"

The Archbishop added: "It was difficult not to scrap my address and try to answer that appeal. I am sure that Wesley would insist that the man who knows in his own personal life the transforming power of Christ is the man who will most ardently believe in, and labor for, the power of Christ to renew and transform the world."

This hymn, written by Miss Katherine Hankey, an Englishwoman, has been translated into many languages, and also set to several tunes. But an American, Dr. W. H. Doane, composed the tune to which it is most frequently sung. Mr. Ira D. Sankey reports Dr. Doane as saying: " I wrote music for the song one hot afternoon while on the stagecoach between the Glen Falls House and the Crawford House in the White Mountains. That evening we sang it in the parlors of the hotel. We thought it pretty, though we scarcely anticipated the popularity which was subsequently accorded it." *

Since the hymn was launched on its career of usefulness, multitudes have enjoyed singing:

> " Tell me the old, old story
> Of unseen things above,
> Of Jesus and His glory,
> Of Jesus and His love."

Ford Played His Hymn on Jew's-Harp

" What is the first hymn you remember? " That was one of the questions which Dr. William L. Stidger once asked Henry Ford during an interview. The answer took an altogether unexpected form, for Dr. Stidger said:

" He took out of his coat pocket a jew's-harp, such as most of us remember playing when youngsters, and started to play the answer to my question. I did not recognize the old hymn at first, so he played it again, more emphatically

* " My Life, and the Story of the Gospel Hymns," by Ira D. Sankey (Harper & Brothers).

and slowly. Then I got it. It was, ' Take It to the Lord in Prayer.' "

" This is the first hymn I remember," commented Mr. Ford.

Thus the inventor, after more than half a century had passed, could recall the days when as a boy he heard sung the story of the friendship of Jesus—

> " What a Friend we have in Jesus,
> All our sins and griefs to bear!
> What a privilege to carry
> Everything to God in prayer.

> .   .   .   .   .   .

> " Have we trials and temptations?
> Is there trouble anywhere?
> We should never be discouraged:
> Take it to the Lord in prayer.
> Can we find a friend so faithful
> Who will all our sorrows share?
> Jesus knows our every weakness:
> Take it to the Lord in prayer."

CHAPTER IV

SOUL TONIC IN SACRED SONG

"My grandmother used to sing hymns when dispirited and often remarked she felt happier. 'They roll the gloom away,' she declared."—*O. O. McIntyre.*

"I find so many songs to sing
I scarce know what to do,
Though I keep singing every hour
I'm never, never through."
—*Helen Loomis Linham in*
"Good Housekeeping."

When Sir Harry Lauder was presented with the freedom of the City of Edinburgh he charmed the audience by breaking into song. He also described how when he "ran into a bank of mist and everything was dark," he turned on the record of "The End of the Road," and listened to himself singing it. As the song continued, he would say to himself, "Well, old man, you will have to take you own advice."—*Selected.*

"She was here last Monday and will come again in two weeks. On the tick of the hour she appears at the door, saying cheerfully, 'Well, how's everybody today? What shall I do first, ma'am?' Then the house grows cleaner to the accompaniment of song, sweet, clear, vibrant. Her work is in the valley but her heart is with the stars.

"'On the Rock of Ages founded,
What can shake thy sure repose?
With salvation's walls surrounded,
Thou may'st smile at all thy foes.'

"As she wrings her mop and begins again, she sings:

" ' Teach me some melodious sonnet,
   Sung by flaming tongues above;
Praise the mount—I'm fixed upon it—
   Mount of Thy redeeming love.'

" She seems to polish the windows more perfectly when she sings! When we spoke of it, she replied, ' Oh, yes, ma'am, our preacher said we could do our everyday work for God, so I shine the windows a bit better because I'm doing it for Him and it makes me happy.' "—*Mary W. Cuykendall, in " The Home Quarterly."*

Editor's " Soul Music on a Rainy Day "

Headed for his office one morning a London editor found himself following a messenger boy, who carried a big bundle under his arm. The sidewalk was narrow, and the traffic was great. So the editor slowed his pace and continued to follow the lad. The boy was whistling with such happy enthusiasm that the editor declared that he could see " his cheeks bulging out in front of his ears. He was whistling a hymn tune. It was raining heavily, which seemed to make him whistle more passionately." The London lad was whistling, as he trudged through the rain with his bundle, the tune which goes with the familiar hymn:

> " My Jesus, I love Thee, I know Thou art mine,
> For Thee all the pleasures of sin I resign;
> My gracious Redeemer, my Saviour art Thou,
> If ever I loved Thee, my Jesus, 'tis now."

With the music on his whistling lips, doubtless the words were runnnig through the mind of the lad. Anyhow, the tune brightened the rainy day for the editor, and he pleasantly recorded the scene in a very delightful way in his editorial columns (which are read in several lands) by saying of the boy: " His whistling of the tune set me humming it, and I, for my part, could not separate the tune from the words. Thus we were walking in a kind of procession: he the band in front; I marching to it. And so, as the Bible says about Lot and Zoar, ' The sun was risen upon the earth ' (see Genesis 19: 23) when I sat down in my chair and faced my correspondence."

Whistling for his own satisfaction, the messenger lad

brought sunshine into the soul of a busy and scholarly man on a day of cloud and rain.

Meeting Made Memorable by an Old Song

Though a comparative stranger in the neighborhood, yet S. W. Grafflin, long a noted worker among young people, attended the mid-week meeting of the church. An interesting description of what happened was afterward related by him. The pastor had made an excellent address, and the singing was better than that heard at most mid-week gatherings, yet the meeting seemed to lack something until the unexpected occurred.

" Suddenly, out of the stillness of the moment, there came the strong, rugged tones of a man's voice, singing, to us at least, a long-forgotten hymn." It was one of the revival songs of a former day:

> " We praise Thee, O God! for the Son of Thy love,
> For Jesus who died, and is now gone above.
>
> " Hallelujah! Thine the glory, Hallelujah! Amen.
> Hallelujah! Thine the glory, revive us again."

The man sang alone for a moment; then he was joined by some of the older members of the group. " When he finished the second stanza, the room was ringing with great singing, and vibrant with something which before had not been present." Immediately people began to give their testimonies; there was more singing; and the meeting was one of joyfulness.

The success of the meeting was later discussed. Being particularly interested in young people, Dr. Grafflin remarked: " I was struck by the reaction of two or three bright youngsters who were there, and by their comments on the voluntary singing; and also the fact that all the older members seemed to know, enjoy, and be able to sing the hymn, even without the music."

Thus happy memories were awakened in the souls of the older people, while the young folks enjoyed the old-time song with its heart-stirring strains of music.

Soul Tonic in a Song

A man drifted into the service at Central Hall ("Sunshine Hall"), London, England, and listened to the singing of Fanny Crosby's poetic message of confidence:

> "Blessed assurance! Jesus is mine!
> Oh what a foretaste of glory divine!"

The day was wet, and the man was discouraged; but soon he was singing with the others:

> "This is my story, this is my song,
> Praising my Saviour all the day long."

"This was just the tonic I needed," said the visitor afterward to one of the workers. The song had brought him "sunshine in the soul."

When someone spoke to Frances Ridley Havergal about the blindness of Fanny Crosby, Miss Havergal promptly replied, "But her heart can see."

"Blessed Assurance" is regarded by some people as being the most impressive of the many sacred songs written by this gifted author. Her friend, Mrs. Joseph F. Knapp, had composed a tune concerning which the blind singer said: "It seemed to me to be one of the sweetest I had heard for a long time." Mrs. Knapp asked Fanny to write a hymn for the tune. The latter confessed that she " felt while bringing the words and tones together that the air and the hymn were intended for each other." That opinion was confirmed after hearing the hymn sung hundreds of times.

Thus, two American women united in furnishing the musical message that proved to be a soul tonic for a depressed Englishman.

" The song is a stirring one," said Dr. Edmund Lorenz (" Practical Hymn Studies "), " its music being full of spirit and vigor; but it will do more than stir the physical pulses, it will reach the spiritual pulse. . . ."

Joyful Companionship

An aged couple from the country were walking slowly down the crowded street of a populous midwestern city. Those observing them were attracted by their rustic garb and the unhurried manner in which they moved. Grayheaded and stoop-shouldered, they peered through their spectacles at the strange sights of the city. Dr. Joseph Clark, long prominent in the work of religious education in the State of New York and elsewhere, saw the couple, and they made a lasting impression on his memory. Many years later he related the incident, and commented on the fact that " the unusual thing about them was that they were holding hands, as doubtless they had done many times before in their married life of half a century."

People smiled as the couple passed; and Dr. Clark confessed that he stepped aside to watch them as they slowly disappeared in the distance. Resuming his journey, he began to think about the beautiful companionship existing

between these two aged people as they together lived the
simple and unaffected life. "Communion with the Eternal," said he, "must be something like that, just walking
hand in hand with God through the years."

Almost unconsciously as he proceeded on his way, Dr.
Clark admitted that he found himself humming some lines
from the old gospel song:

> "I've reached the land of corn and wine,
> And all its riches freely mine."

But the words which were in his mind that day, and ready
to fall from his lips were those of the second verse of
"Beulah Land":

> "My Saviour comes and walks with me,
> And sweet communion here have we;
> He gently leads me by His hand,
> For this is heaven's borderland."

Sang His Speech

Church anniversary occasions in England are times of
rejoicing. Home-comings, sermons, speeches and tea-meet-
ings feature the happy days. Then, if ever, crowds are in
attendance.

The Albert Hall of Nottingham, in the early part of
1936, was filled with five hundred people beyond its seat-
ing capacity for its anniversary exercises. Mr. Edmund S.
Lamplough, who was at that time the Vice President of
the Methodist Conference, presided over the platform
meeting. The chairman's speech is always a matter of peculiar interest. But Mr. Lamplough, a local preacher and
a musician, quite surprised his audience by stating that he

intended to sing his speech. What would he sing? The question soon was answered when he sang from " The Methodist Hymn Book," issued three years earlier:

> " Will your anchor hold in the storms of life,
> Will the clouds unfold their wings of strife?
> When the strong tides lift, and the cables strain,
> Will your anchor drift, or firm remain? "

The singer sang the four verses, concluding with:

> " Will your eyes behold through the morning light
> The city of gold and the harbor bright?
> Will you anchor safe by the heavenly shore,
> When life's storms are past forevermore? "

At the close of each verse the three thousand men and women present joined in the refrain:

> " We have an anchor that keeps the soul
> Steadfast and sure while the billows roll;
> Fastened to the Rock which cannot move,
> Grounded firm and deep in the Saviour's love."

The author of this hymn, Miss Priscilla Jane Owens, a public school teacher in Baltimore, was of Scotch and Welsh descent. For fifty years she was actively engaged in Sunday-school work, and for Sunday schools and young people most of her songs were written.

Making the Soul a Singing-Bird

> " Angels holy,
> High and lowly,
> Sing the praises of the Lord!
> Earth and sky; all living nature;
> Man, the stamp of thy Creator,
> Praise ye, praise ye God the Lord! "

John Stuart Blackie, the cultured and beloved professor of Greek in the University of Edinburgh for many years, expressed his attitude toward life in these lines. Born in Glasgow in 1809, he lived to a ripe age. He was giving lectures on Scotch Songs in England at the age of eighty-two. This happy-hearted man once said of himself: " I am rather a young old boy and I am one of the happiest creatures under the sun at this moment, and my amusement is to sing songs. . . . I advise you to do the same. Your soul will become a singing-bird, and then the Devil won't get near it." On another occasion he said: " At home I am always singing Scotch songs." Concerning this scholar, who also was a member of the bar and the son of a banker, Dr. Charles S. Robinson has stated that he had become " widely known in almost every field of literature, poetry and prose, and noted for his force and brilliancy of thought."

The last stanza of the joyous hymn of this man with the singing soul indicated his great desire that others should join him in forming a group of singing-birds to sound the praises of God. Said he in his poetic lines:

> " Praise Him ever,
> Bounteous Giver;
> Praise Him, Father, Friend and Lord!
> Each glad soul its free course winging,
> Each glad voice its free song singing,
> Praise the great and mighty Lord! "

What a life of happiness and rejoicing this world would be if Christians followed the wise counsel of this man with the singing heart! " This is one of the noblest bits of nature-painting in literature," W. T. Stead quotes an English minister as saying. And he stated that the hymn was sent to him by one who had been cheered by the song as by a sea-breeze. Then he added: " It is the nineteenth-century version of the sentiment which Milton expressed in the seventeenth, and Addison in the eighteenth, each in the mode of his day and generation."

The editor of " The Student Hymnary " included this in his collection in 1937. " The Hymnal " (Presbyterian) places the hymn under the heading of " God the Father," and under the division of " God in Nature."

Found the Needed Message

A teacher of a Bible class earned his living by tuning and repairing pianos in his native England. On one occasion there came to him a time of severe testing. During that period, while he was greatly perplexed in his mind, he was given the job of thoroughly overhauling a piano. Working away with painstaking patience, he took it carefully apart. Reaching the base, he noticed a piece of paper glued to the wood.

Curious to learn what was on this, he found the words of a well-known chorus—" Trusting Jesus, that is all."

The man began to think of the gospel song of which this was a part. Soon he found himself repeating the lines:

" Simply trusting every day,
    Trusting thro' a stormy way;
Even when my faith is small,
    Trusting Jesus, that is all.

    " Trusting as the moments fly,
        Trusting as the days go by;
    Trusting Him whate'er befall,
        Trusting Jesus, that is all."

The message of the song came to the man's soul in a time of great need, and it proved to be sustainingly sufficient. Now he was able to sing:

> " Singing if my way be clear:
>   Praying if my path be drear:
> If in danger, for Him call;
>   Trusting Jesus, that is all."

CHAPTER V

SONGS OF THE HANDICAPPED

Hamilton, Ont., March 17—(AP). The hymn, "Nearer, My God, to Thee," will be sung in sign language by members of the deaf and dumb mission here, in paying tribute to Mrs. Sarah Jane Greer Irvine, mother of St. John Irvine, noted dramatist and novelist, at her burial today. Mrs. Irvine, who was deaf and dumb, came here from Ireland 18 years ago.—*From the Associated Press, March, 1931.*

"Years ago a blind Chinese girl, with a voice of deep human sympathy, was singing in our Chinese rescue home in San Francisco. Her sad life had been reclaimed. She knew her Lord, and scarcely an eye was dry as she sweetly sang:

" ' Once I was blind, but now I can see;
The light of the world is Jesus.' "
—From an article by John Timothy Stone, D.D., in the " Watertown Times."

"Passing through Gary, Indiana, last summer, I thought of the little crippled newsboy who, years ago, gave his life there to save the life of a young girl unknown to him. Billy Rugh had willingly undergone great suffering in the belief that he might save her, hoping, of course, to keep his own life; but when he saw that he was to die, he said cheerfully, ' I have been of some use after all.'

" Fifteen thousand mourners stood there listening and singing:

" ' Nearer, my God, to Thee.'

The little crippled child had brought them all nearer to God."
—Frederick K. Stamm, D.D., in " Good Housekeeping," August, 1937.

81

Blind Soldiers Sang " Lead, Kindly Light "

Most touching was the scene when two hundred blind men sang " Lead, Kindly Light " at the funeral of one of the most famous blind men in history.

Sir Arthur Pearson, who died in London on December 9th, 1921, achieved success early in life. His influence was wide-spread. He became the owner of the *Daily Express,* the *Morning* and *Evening Standard,* and also a chain of papers in various sections of England. Gradually, however, he became blind. Therefore in 1910 he retired from newspaper work, and soon began to show others how they could overcome some of the handicaps of blindness.

Various parts of the British Empire were represented by the men who were taken to London within a short period after the World War began in 1914. Sir Arthur Pearson was the one man who could most help them. So he founded St. Dunstan's in London, which became a famous hospital for blinded soldiers. There they were taught to read Braille. The whole problem of readjustment to the new conditions of life was faced; and before the end of 1918 over six hundred men had already " learned to be blind," and nearly seven hundred more remained in training at St. Dunstan's. Two hundred additional men were still in various hospitals. Sir Arthur himself, in 1919, told a part of this story in his book, " Victory Over Blindness."

Each of these men had been met personally by Sir Arthur on their return from the front. A watch, which was made specially for the blind, was presented to every man. This watch " had dots to indicate the place of the ordinary numerals and hands slightly raised, and so strong that their position could be safely felt with the fingers." Soon, also, in addition to learning Braille, they began to use typewriters, and likewise to do many other things of a useful nature. Eventually they were fitted to return to their homes and earn a living—in some cases better than they before earned. Throughout their period of readjustment, the men were encouraged by the knowledge that Sir Arthur could tell them, from his own experience, how they could win the victory over blindness. He was deservedly honored by the King for his work among the blind.

Those blind men who were singing on that December day beside the grave of their friend had come from all parts of England. They had selected their own hymn; and those sightless victims of the Great War were singing out of their hearts because of the man whose memory they reverently cherished. Was not their song also a prayer for themselves? Nothing like it was ever before witnessed. This incident alone would have made Newman's immortal hymn memorable in modern life. Two hundred blind men, some of whom had to travel far to be present, sang around the grave of a common friend and helper:

> "Lead, kindly Light, amid the encircling gloom,
>   Lead Thou me on!
> The night is dark, and I am far from home;
>   Lead Thou me on!
> Keep Thou my feet . . ."

"There was not a dry eye in Hampstead Cemetery," the Rev. F. Hoggarth, an English writer, has told us, as the spectators saw the group of blind men, and then heard their appealing song.

Singing amid the darkness of earth's life, the singers closed with lines of song which hopefully expressed the thought that there would come a golden morning when

they would see "face to face" the man whose memory
they cherished, when

> ". . . with the morn those angel faces smile;
> Which I have loved long since, and lost a while!"

Crippled Children Sang for Their Doctor

One of the ablest practitioners of orthopedic surgery
was Sir Robert Jones of Liverpool, England. He was characterized as "one of those Welsh geniuses who have
placed the whole world in their debt." Making an an-
nouncement of his death early in 1933, at the age of
seventy-four, an American periodical stated that "he was
honored in his lifetime by the universities of two hemi-
spheres, and by many governments . . . for his hospital
service in the World War." Said the Bishop of Liverpool
at the memorial service for this good physician:

"If in this city and other cities far fewer cripples are
to be seen today than forty years ago, if a new power has
come to enrich and enable the healing and restoring art,
then it is through him more than any other man that it
was received and given. He showed and he shared the
spirit of the pioneer." In one hospital the children used to
sing for him:

> "Now the day is over,
>   Night is drawing nigh,
> Shadows of the evening
>   Steal across the sky."

Sir Robert loved little children, and they loved him. He
became the hero of hundreds of boys and girls whose

limbs he had made straight. Thus they loved to sing a special arrangement of the second verse:

" Give to cripples' doctors
Calm and sweet repose;
With the children's blessing
May their eyelids close."

The assembly at his funeral were moved to tears when the youngest choir boy, unaccompanied, sang this verse " from the elevated ' Resting ' in the great cathedral where his ashes had been deposited."

The song of the crippled children for their doctor was an expression of their gratitude to him and also a prayer for him.

Lepers Sang Whittier's Hymn

" We may not climb the heavenly steeps
To bring the Lord Christ down."

An American went to the leper colony in Porto Rico and found the lepers assembled for a religious service in the clinic, which was the only available place. Said Coe Williams, as he described the surroundings in an article in *The Christian Advocate:* " We passed down the avenue of whitewashed walls and cool, lacy bamboo shadows— for the lepers had asked us to be there at two o'clock."

Near the building, the voices of lepers were heard, as they rang out through the windows of the clinic. These afflicted people were singing. The Christian message had changed their lives. Most appropriately they sang the words of Whittier:

> " But warm, sweet, tender, even yet
>   A present help is He;
> And faith has still its Olivet,
>   And love its Galilee.

> " The healing of His seamless dress
>   Is by our beds of pain. . . ."

Doubtless the lepers were thinking of the Christ who healed people afflicted as they were, when He " was here among men." Also, they knew that those who were serving them were ministering in the name of Him who is

> " Lord and Master of us all."

The Blind Girl's " Good Shepherd "

The " guest preacher " had an impressively pleasant experience which he afterward related for the enjoyment of his friends. A young woman, blind from birth, was announced to render a solo. " Her radiant face and cheery smile captivated the members of the congregation." Listeners wondered what her selection would be. The people, however, were " deeply stirred when the blind girl gave a wonderful interpretation of the music set " to the hymn of Henry Williams Baker:

> " The King of love my Shepherd is,
>   Whose goodness faileth never;
> I nothing lack if I am His
>   And He is mine forever."

Blind, yet she was assured of the fact that she would be cared for by the Good Shepherd! " Oh, the sustaining power of such tremendous faith! " exclaimed the minister who had heard the blind girl sing.

From the sweet voice and the happy soul came the words of assurance with which the hymn closes:

" And so through all the length of days,
Thy goodness faileth never;
Great Shepherd, may I sing Thy praise
Within Thy house forever."

This hymn, dated 1868, is " considered by some as the most beautiful of all the metrical versions of the Twenty-third Psalm." Dr. John B. Dykes wrote for this hymn his " lovely melody ' Dominus Regit Me,' " which, says Robinson, " is as fine as the hymn."

The last words which the friends of the author heard him utter were those of the third stanza:

" Perverse and foolish oft I strayed,
But yet in love He sought me,
And on His shoulder gently laid,
And home, rejoicing, brought me."

" This tender sadness," says Dr. Julian, " brightened by a soft, calm peace, was an epitome of his poetical life." " Both hymn and tune were sung at Dr. Dyke's funeral on January 28, 1876 " (Covert and Laufer).

What an appropriate selection the blind girl made for her song!

CHAPTER VI

SINGING SEAMEN

" Sing unto the Lord a new song, . . . ye that go down to the sea." *(Isa. 42: 10.)*

" The deep roar of the ocean as it beats against the rocks, the thundering oratorio of the cataract, the crash of the storm, ' the music of the spheres '—these are nature's major chords."
—*The Rev. Elmer E. Helms, D.D.*

" The six Scottish fishermen, who were recently drowned in the Aberdeen steam trawler *Rosslyn,* were heard singing hymns in the wheelhouse of the vessel just before the high seas washed them overboard. I should like to know what they sang then. I do not think that their singing ended that day as they went to their ocean grave!"—*The Right Hon. Isaac Foot,* in an address, November, 1937.

" There are few times when Wesley's hymn—

" ' With faith I plunge me in this sea;
Here is my hope, my joy, my rest,'

so thrills as when sung by a congregation of these old sea stalwarts, the Shetlanders, who a few hours before the service were riding tumultuous seas in little craft of less than thirty tons."
—*F. B. H., in " The Methodist Recorder."*

" We were coming back from France on a transport," wrote a clergyman who had ministered to American soldiers during the World War, " and it was against the rules to allow a civilian to come unless he was assigned to some duty. The captain politely explained this rule to me and then assigned me to keep a watch every night on the aft gun deck just like a regular army man.

" I was assigned the eight-to-midnight watch on the aft gun

88

deck. Below me were two big guns, with two boys assigned to each and two in reserve. I used to pace that deck and hear those boys singing the old hymns of the Church. One night in a beastly storm I heard them singing softly through the tumult (I never heard that hymn sung when it meant so much to me):

> " ' Jesus, Saviour, pilot me
> Over life's tempestuous sea;
> Unknown waves before me roll,
> Hiding rock and treacherous shoal;
> Chart and compass came from Thee;
> Jesus, Saviour, pilot me.

> " ' As a mother stills her child,
> Thou canst hush the ocean wild;
> Boisterous waves obey Thy will
> When Thou sayest to them, " Be still! "
> Wondrous Sovereign of the sea,
> Jesus, Saviour, pilot me.' "

Midshipmen at Chapel Service

A description of the Sunday chapel service at the Naval Academy at Annapolis appeared in an article in *The Boys' World,* written by P. H. V. Weems, Jr., Midshipman, U. S. N. The service, he indicated, follows the order of the Episcopal Church. Following formation, " with all hands wearing full dress uniforms and white gloves, . . . the drum and bugle corps strikes up a lively fanfare and marches off. The companies swing into line and follow directly behind." When the chapel is reached, " the drum and bugle corps faces about in front of the broad steps and continues playing until the entire regiment is in the chapel." The regular naval chaplain presides over the service. The author of the article said:

" The close of the service is especially impressive, because it is always concluded by singing the first stanza of ' For Those in Peril on the Sea,' with the entire congregation kneeling. The verse is sung softly by the midshipmen and is very moving to them and the visitors as well, because it so directly applies to the lives and officers of men in the service. It is quoted here:

> " ' Eternal Father, strong to save,
> Whose arm hath bound the restless wave,
> Who bidd'st the mighty ocean deep
> Its own appointed limits keep:
> O hear us when we cry to Thee
> For those in peril on the sea.'

" When the song is ended the regiment marches out in the same manner that it marched in, and is dismissed in front of the chapel."

Most appropriate for the occasion are the lines thus sung.

Melody and Duty

Members of the band of the Salvation Army of Hythe, England, were in their citadel playing on a summer evening in 1935. Among other selections they played the hymn so well known to all seamen—

> " Eternal Father, strong to save,
>   Whose arm hath bound the restless wave,
>   Who bidd'st the mighty ocean deep
>   Its own appointed limits keep:
>   O hear us when we cry to Thee
>   For those in peril on the sea."

Said an English periodical, " Suddenly a deep boom broke through the music. The warning of a ship in distress was given, and the lifeboat men were being called to duty. Many of the bandsmen were members of the crew, and they immediately downed their instruments and rushed off to the lifeboat station."

Within seven minutes from the time the call sounded, the lifeboat was on its way to " rescue the perishing." A mile out in the channel a fishing boat was drifting helplessly. But the men who had been making music on their instruments a short time before, and who responded instantly to the call of duty, had the joy of aiding those in distress. Having prayed on their instruments " for those in peril on the sea," they were ready to answer their own prayers.

> " Thus evermore shall rise to Thee
>   Glad hymns of praise from land and sea."

" Sir, the Song Did It "

Two ministers, the Rev. W. Y. Fullerton and the Rev. Manton Smith, used to conduct evangelistic meetings together. *The Christian Herald* (London) reported the incident of a time when these two evangelists were at work in the West of Scotland. One day Mr. Smith engaged a rowing boat in order to make a trip to one of the islands, and wandered about among the rocks until it was time to return.

When, however, the boatman started to row back he realized that he was facing a contrary wind, and so he was able to make little progress. The minister encouraged the boatman in his persistent efforts. Then, while the latter was laboring at the oars, the minister began to sing the chorus of an old gospel song, written by the evangelistic singer, P. P. Bliss:

> " Pull for the shore, sailor, pull for the shore!
> Heed not the rolling waves, but bend to the oar."

The mainland was reached after a vigorous effort, and as minister and sailor stepped out of the boat, the latter said to Mr. Smith: " Sir, it was the song that did it! "

Thus the song of the American singer, which began:

> " Light in the darkness, sailor, day is at hand! "

and which a former generation sang with zestful delight, aided in the rescue of two men on the other side of the Atlantic from the perils of the ocean.

Unseen Singers on the Sea

Excitement and curiosity were aroused by passengers on a ship that had been out of sight of land for almost ten days when it was learned that a call was to be made at Pitcairn Island. The story was related by a writer from New Zealand, a lady, in *The British Weekly,* who mentioned this "lonely little island" as being "two miles long and one mile broad, with its highest part 1,000 feet above sea level, with about 260 inhabitants, and a history as romantic as was ever penned."

The opening of the Panama Canal resulted in the direct trade route passing this island, yet vessels stop there but seldom. But when they do so, the natives come out in their boats to barter fruit and curios.

This particular ship had kerosene and other useful things for residents of the island; but as the weather was unfavorable, the boat stopped two miles from the coast. The night was dark; but responding to the call of the ship small lights were quickly seen bobbing on the waters, and voices were heard. Soon about twenty men and women were climbing the rope ladders hanging from the side of the boat. They had with them various bundles and baskets, as well as fruit. After bartering with crew and passengers for two hours, the time came for the visitors to leave. But, reaching their small boats, and pulling away from the big ship, the departing visitors began to sing in beautiful harmony—

"There's a land that is fairer than day,
And by faith we can see it afar;
For the Father waits over the way,
To prepare us a dwelling-place there.

" In the sweet by and by,
    We shall meet on that beautiful shore;
In the sweet by and by,
    We shall meet on that beautiful shore."

" It was extraordinarily touching," said the writer, " and as they disappeared in the darkness to their home two miles away we felt that we would not readily have missed the evening's experience."

Fishermen Guided Through Fog

A visitor to the quaint seaside town of St. Ives, Cornwall, England, gleaned a lovely story which he contributed to *The Christian Herald*, London. Many of the men of the community were engaged in fishing, and the visitor watched them with great interest. One day he walked down to the beach at a time when a heavy fog prevailed, and witnessed something which captivated his attention. Said he: " On a little headland a number of fishermen's wives and daughters were gathered together singing hymns. I asked the women the reason for this singing, and they replied that the fishermen, being unable to see in the dense fog, might be lost; but they learned their position from that of the singers, and could guide their little boats by the singing." One of the selections which they sang was Fanny Crosby's familiar song. First the women sang:

" Safe in the arms of Jesus,
    Safe on His gentle breast,
There by His love o'ershaded,
    Sweetly my soul shall rest."

Then the fishermen, catching the strains of music as it came over the waves, answered in song:

> " Hark 'tis the voice of angels
> Borne in a song to me,
> Over the fields of glory,
> Over the jasper sea."

" I was entranced," said the visitor. " The whole place seemed to be holy ground."

This song was written for the tune. Dr. W. H. Doane told Fanny Crosby that he had composed a tune, and would like words for the same. When she heard it played, she said, " Why that tune says, ' Safe in the arms of Jesus.' " She retired to an adjoining room, and Mr. Sankey tells us that in thirty minutes she returned with her gospel song, which was soon translated into several foreign languages.

" Jesus, Saviour, Pilot Me "

Being taken ill while on a visit to Kingston, Canada, Professor T. R. Glover, of Cambridge University, became a patient in a hospital. Later, in Toronto, Professor Glover delivered an address to a group of young people, and indicated that his room when in the hospital at Kingston was very high. He could see little but the St. Lawrence River. Listening to the steamers, he heard the calls which signalled for the pilots to come aboard to guide the vessels through the perils of the great river.

Jesus Christ, the scholarly speaker affirmed, is the pilot of human lives throughout their entire course. The young people, he suggested, should pray, " Pilot, Pilot, come aboard! " To Him they should commit the guidance of their lives.

This very thought finds expression in a beloved hymn:

> " Jesus, Saviour, pilot me
> Over life's tempestuous sea;
> Unknown waves before me roll,
> Hiding rock and treacherous shoal;
> Chart and compass came from Thee;
> Jesus, Saviour, pilot me."

The author of this hymn knew much about the sea, for he was born and educated in the City of New York, and with the exception of eleven years, during which he was pastor at Sag Harbor, Long Island, all his ministry was spent in his native city. For seventeen years he was the minister of the *Church of the Sea and Land* in New York; and of this church the Rev. Edwin Hopper, D.D., the writer of this hymn, was the pastor when he was suddenly translated. He had just finished some lines on " Heaven," when his pencil dropped on the manuscript before him. The prayer found in the closing lines of the hymn had been answered:

> " When at last I near the shore,
>
> .   .   .   .   .
>
> May I hear Thee say to me,
> ' Fear not, I will pilot thee.' "

This hymn was first published in the *Sailors' Magazine* (for he preached regularly to many seamen) in 1871. Dr. Hopper lived seventy fruitful years—1818–1888. His hymn " has become deservedly popular, not only with seagoing folk, but with all voyagers on the sea of life."

Scotch Fishermen at an English Service

A lovely story of Scottish fisherfolk was related in the *Eastern Daily Express* (in England) which told how those fishermen spent a Sunday in the mid-thirties of our own century. Those men sturdily refused to go fishing on Sunday, no matter how great the catch might possibly be. So the men, who were fishing off the English coast, spent a Sunday at Yarmouth.

There they attended a religious service in the Church of St. Nicholas, of the Church of England. When the rector announced the Scripture lesson those fisherfolk from the North took their Bibles from their pockets and followed the reading.

"Everything in that service was right," it was remarked. Someone sang as a solo the song of Charles H. Gabriel—

> "Upon a wide and stormy sea
> Thou'rt sailing to eternity,
> And thy great Adm'ral orders thee:—
> Sail on! sail on! sail on!"

The men listened with keenest delight, and their enjoyment was pictured on their faces as the soloist came to the chorus:

> "Sail on! sail on! the storm will soon be past
> The darkness will not always last;
> Sail on! sail on! God lives and He commands:
> Sail on! sail on!"

Someone remarked that this service was "an altogether delightful thing even to read about; and what must it have been to be there!"

Wesley Encouraged Sailors with Song

Desiring to make a trip to the Scilly Islands during one of his preaching missions in Cornwall, John Wesley engaged some fishermen of St. Ives to take him from the mainland to the Islands, a distance of about forty-five miles. Soon after they started a furious storm arose, and the high waves rolling in from the broad Atlantic threatened to swamp the little boat.

Thinking it impossible to make the trip with safety, the seamen decided that they ought to return. Wesley, however, anxious to reach his destination, sought to encourage the men to proceed. Most lustily, therefore, he began to sing some lines from a hymn familiar to them, and which still finds favor with English congregations:

> " Peace, doubting heart! my God's I am:
> Who formed me man, forbids my fear."

The second stanza of the hymn was especially appropriate for such a time as this. Hence the great religious leader soon was singing for the fishermen the lines which would have for them a special appeal:

> " When, passing through the watery deep,
> I ask in faith His promised aid,
> The waves an awful distance keep
> And shrink from my devoted head:
> Fearless their violence I dare;
> They cannot harm, for God is there."

Encouraged by the message of song, the sailors exerted all their strength, and all reached the Scilly Islands in safety.

CHAPTER VII

MISSIONARIES AND MUSIC

" Sing unto the Lord, all the earth." *(I Chron. 16: 23.)*

" Watchman, tell us of the night,
What its signs of promise are.
Traveler, o'er yon mountain's height
See that glory-beaming star!
Watchman, does its beauteous ray
Aught of joy or hope foretell?
Traveler, yes; it brings the day,
Promised day of Israel."

This beloved missionary hymn was published by Sir John Bowring in 1825. Very singularly, however, the author did not hear it sung for ten years. He is reported to have told a friend in China that he first heard it sung in Asiatic Turkey sometime in 1835 when he attended a prayer meeting of American missionaries, and they sang the hymn he had written.

Chaplain (later Bishop) C. C. McCabe visited a Methodist Conference in Iowa in 1870. Bishop Edward R. Ames, who was presiding, suggested that business be suspended while Chaplain McCabe sang. Going to the organ, McCabe began to play and sing a hymn which had been written just four years earlier by Miss Katherine Hankey, a young Englishwoman. The song was new to most of the ministers, and they listened with delight while the visitor sang:

" I love to tell the story
Of unseen things above,
Of Jesus and His glory,
Of Jesus and His love."

99

"Many of us had never heard the song or the singer," wrote one of the ministers present. "I sat in the 'Amen' corner where I could see the people well, and noticed in a little while that they were being deeply moved—and soon about all of them were weeping. . . . The bishop said next morning, 'I have heard the Chaplain sing that song half a dozen times, and I cried every time.'"

Singing When the Angels Took Charge

They called themselves "The Trio," and well they might. Together they formed a threefold cord, and thus they were able to lend support to each other. "The Trio" consisted of three women who went as missionaries under the China Inland Mission. Back in England for furlough in 1933, they had, between them, spent ninety-seven years in mission work in China. Their names have become widely known—Mildred Cable and Francesca and Evangeline French. Their experiences thrilled great English audiences when related. And the story of this combination of personalities has been told in "Something Happened," * which is "in part an autobiography and in part a record of amazingly heroic endeavor and accomplishment." For twenty-one years they did remarkable educational work in Shansi. Later they labored as itinerant evangelists among the untouched tribes; and at Suchow, "The City of Prodigals," they had their winter quarters.

Among the many incidents recorded is that of the time when they were surrounded by fierce robbers. The women were in their sleeping tent. Outside the bandits sat around the campfire with their polished guns. But "The Trio" "were conscious of the wall of fire which encircled them. After a while they slept, and the angels took charge."

The Psalmist knew that when the angels take charge God's people are secure. The experiences of Peter and Paul afford similar testimony. "The Trio" had a hymn which they sang nightly under every circumstance. How appropriate it must have been! Perhaps it enabled them to realize more vividly that the angels would take charge,

* China Inland Mission, Philadelphia, Pa.

even though the bandits surrounded them. This was their song:

> " Guide me, O Thou great Jehovah,
>   Pilgrim through this barren land;
> I am weak, but Thou art mighty;
>   Hold me with Thy powerful hand."

Courage was combined with faith as they sang on that unforgetable night:

> " Strong Deliverer,
>   Be Thou still my Strength and Shield."

Christmas Day was once spent in captivity among robbers. Their Christmas dinner consisted of some hard, dried crusts of bread and a little tea! After such a Christmas dinner it was heroic for the little group to sing at eventide:

> " Bread of heaven,
>   Feed me till I want no more."

Undiscouraged by their testing experiences, they found that God gave them the singing spirit amid all conditions. Out of their " stony griefs " " The Trio " blended their voices night after night, and the last songful words before retiring were praiseful:

> " Songs of praises
> I will ever give to Thee."

Livingstone's Favorite Hymn

The favorite hymn of David Livingstone was sung at his funeral " beneath the arches of Westminster Abbey,

April 18, 1874," when his body, which had been carried by the loving hands of those whom he loved and served, was brought back to England's national shrine to rest in honor. Amid his wilderness journeyings in Africa the hymn which sustained his soul was one which had been written by Philip Doddridge, the author of at least three hundred and seventy hymns:

> " O God of Bethel by whose hand
> Thy people still are fed;
> Who through this weary pilgrimage
> Hast all our fathers led!

> " Our vows, our prayers, we now present
> Before Thy throne of grace;
> God of our fathers! be the God
> Of their succeeding race."

This hymn, said S. R. Crockett, "makes men and women square themselves and stand erect to sing, like an army that goes gladly to battle." When King George V observed his jubilee this hymn was included in the King's Silver Jubilee form of Prayer and Thanksgiving held in St. Paul's Cathedral, London, May 6, 1935. Not only was it sung and heard in the historic and venerable temple of worship, but many thousands of people in the stands outside, listening to the broadcast by loud speakers, heard the reverent words, and great crowds in the streets joined in singing them on that memorable occasion.

A Scotch mission-teacher at Kuruman, Bechuanaland, South Africa, wrote this letter which has been preserved for us by W. T. Stead: " This hymn stands out pre-eminently as the hymn which has helped me beyond all others. It shines with radiant lustre like the star that outshineth all others among the midnight constellations. It has been my solace and comfort in times of trouble, my cheer in times of joy; it is woven into the warp and woof of my spiritual being; its strains were the first I was taught to lisp, and, God helping me, they shall be the last. Sung to the tune of ' Dundee,' that was the refrain of happy meetings or sad partings. Its strains rang out the Old Year and heralded the New. It was chanted as a farewell dirge when I left my home in Scotland. . . .

" I am penning this in the little room that was once the study of David Livingstone, whose walls have often re-echoed to many a strain of praise and supplication, but to none more inspiring and enduring than ' O God of Bethel.' "

Dr. C. S. Robinson tells us that Dr. Doddridge wrote this hymn to be sung after a sermon which he preached on " Jacob's Vow " (Genesis 28: 20–22) on January 16, 1737. A resident of Northampton, where Dr. Doddridge long served as minister and also conducted a training school for young ministers, said in *The British Weekly*, in 1935, that " the hymn was undoubtedly written in the little vestry attached to the old Castle Hill meeting house —a shrine preserved today in much the same condition as when Doddridge used it."

John Logan (1748–1788) revised the hymn and somewhat changed its sentiment. As originally written it began:

> " O God of Jacob, by whose hand
>   Thine Israel still is fed,
> Who through this weary pilgrimage
>   Hath all our fathers led."

And the last stanza in the original ran as follows:

" To Thee, as to our Covenant God
We will ourselves resign;
And count, that not a tenth alone,
But all we have is Thine."

Livingstone's favorite hymn is one which belongs to the ages. The missionary could sing it amid the African solitude; and the multitude assembled in London sang it when they had their great day of rejoicing and thanksgiving at the Silver Jubilee of King George V.

" To Distant Climes the Tidings Bear "

Near the middle of the nineteenth century a young minister was being assisted at a missionary service by the pastor of a neighboring church. This young minister was born in St. Lawrence County, New York, and received his missionary call in the same county. The choir of the little country church at Lawrenceville followed the stirring address of the visiting minister with a hymn—

" Ye Christian heralds, go proclaim
Salvation through Emmanuel's Name;
To distant climes the tidings bear,
And plant the Rose of Sharon there."

Immediately the young pastor was impressed with the fact that the message of the hymn was for him. Said he: " The thought appalled me, and I began to think of difficulties and dangers to be encountered, and to say, ' Impossible! ' " Choir and congregation were soon singing the next stanza:

" God shield you with a wall of fire,
   With flaming zeal your breasts inspire,
Bid raging winds their fury cease,
And hush the tempests into peace."

The great acceptance was made. Said the young minister: " I then and there surrendered myself to God. From that time I had no doubt that God had chosen me for the work." Soon after the Methodist Episcopal Church asked for two young men for India; and the Rev. J. L. Humphrey (who later qualified as a Doctor of Medicine) left Malone, where he was then pastor, for India. The words of the Rev. A. B. Leonard, D.D., at the time of the death of Dr. Humphrey, indicate the significant part he played in the development of missionary activity. Said Dr. Leonard: " *He baptized our first convert in our Indian Mission* and lived to see a membership in Southern Asia of more than 250,000. There are very few men in Christian history who have lived to witness such wonderful results during a single lifetime."

Four terms were served in India by Dr. Humphrey— a total of twenty-four years. He died in Little Falls, New York, September 5, 1910, and the writer attended his funeral in Utica.

This hymn does not find a prominent place in our hymnals, but it is included in " The Hymnal " (Presbyterian), published in Philadelphia in 1933. Its author, the Rev. Bourne H. Draper, was born in Cumnor, near Oxford, England, in 1775, and became a Baptist minister. Also, he was the author of many books. Covert and Laufer (" Handbook to The Hymnal ") make this comment: " The characterization of missionaries as Christian heralds is true to the vocabulary of the gospel commission. Since we are his (Christ's) witnesses how can we think

of our rank among men other than Christian heralds?
The hymn is used rarely except in America."

The hymn of the English Baptist minister led the young
Methodist minister to volunteer for India; and in that
distant country this same minister baptized the first convert of the denomination which he represented. Thus the
ministry of sacred song is far-reaching.

Poetic Mother of a Missionary Son

" As to my history it is soon told: a sinner saved by
grace and sanctified by trials." Thus wrote Mrs. Phoebe
Hinsdale Brown to a minister who sought information
concerning her life. Yet she gave to the Christian Church
a hymn which breathes the deep spirit of meditation; and
her son, the Rev. S. R. Brown, D.D., became the first
Christian missionary from America to Japan, and went to
that country under the auspices of the Reformed (Dutch)
Church. Writing in 1911, Nutter and Tillett said: " Two
of Mrs. Brown's grandchildren are now missionaries in
Japan."

Left an orphan at the age of two, Phoebe Hinsdale did
not learn to read until she was eighteen years of age.
Slight had been her educational advantages when she became the wife of a house painter. Her birthplace was
Canaan, New York (May 1, 1783); but after her mar-
riage she went to live in Ellington, Connecticut; and later
to Monson, Massachusetts. Living in a small unfinished
house, with a sick sister in the only finished room, she
was busy with the care of her four children. Said she:
" There was not a place above or below, where I could
retire for devotion." But at eventide she would go into
an adjacent grove for quiet meditation. The purpose of

these visits was misunderstood, and one day a neighbor, whose garden was near the little grove of trees, reproached her by saying, " If you want anything, why don't you come in and ask for it? "

Said Mrs. Brown: " I went home, and that evening was left alone. After my children were all in bed except my baby, I sat down in my kitchen with my child in my arms, when the grief of my heart burst forth in a flood of tears. I took pen and paper and gave vent to my oppressed heart in what I called ' My Apology for My Twilight Rambles, Addressed to a Lady.' "

From circumstances such as these came the hymn—

> " I love to steal awhile away
> From every cumbering care,
> And spend the hours of closing day
> In humble, grateful prayer."

Mrs. Brown lived for almost thirty years in Monson, after leaving Ellington. She died, however, in Illinois, October 10, 1861; but she was buried in Monson. During her residence in Monson, Mrs. Brown had a large " infant class " in the Sunday school; and she prepared lessons for children that were published by the Massachusetts Sunday-school Society. Her son once wrote to a Mr. Damon, of the Sandwich Islands, who sought information concerning the life and writings of Mrs. Brown, a letter from Yokohoma, Japan, in which he thus referred to his mother: " Her record is on high, and she is with the Lord, whom she loved and served as faithfully as any person I ever knew. . . . To her I owe all that I am; and if I have done any good in the world, to her, under God, it is due. She seems now to have me in her hands, hold-

ing me up to work for Christ and his cause with a grasp
that I can feel."

The meditative and poetic mother, therefore, had much
to do with the making of her missionary son.

Nine verses are found in the original hymn, which
opens with these lines, which are of a touchingly personal nature:

> " Yes, when the toilsome day is gone,
>   And night with banners gray,
> Steals silently the glade along
>   In twilight's soft array,

> " I love to steal awhile away
>   From little ones and care,
> And spend the hours of setting day
>   In gratitude and prayer."

Thus did she write in the eighth verse of her " twilight
rambles ":

> " I love this silent twilight hour
>   Far better than the rest;
> It is, of all the twenty-four,
>   The happiest and the best."

A lovely stanza closed the poem, and this has been
retained by editors of hymnals—

> " Thus, when life's toilsome day is o'er,
>   May its departing ray
> Be calm as this impressive hour,
>   And lead to endless day."

Missionaries Sang When Confronted by Death

" God's peace came into our hearts," the Rev. R. W. Porteous told a vast audience in Kingsway Hall, London, in the spring of 1931, as he related the story of the capture of himself and wife by brigands in China.

These workers of the China Inland Mission were frequently threatened with death. Once they were led to a lonely spot on a hill, and an officer said, " This is the place! " The executioner took his knife from his shoulder; and the courageous couple, expecting immediate death, began to sing:

> " Face to face with Christ my Saviour,
> Face to face—what will it be?
> When with rapture I behold Him,
> Jesus Christ who died for me.

> " Face to face shall I behold Him,
> Far beyond the starry sky;
> Face to face in all His glory,
> I shall see Him by and by! "

After singing their song of hope, should the executioner do his worst, they then sang a hymn which furnished the ground of their confidence:

> " Peace, perfect peace, in this dark world of sin?
> The blood of Jesus whispers peace within.
>
> .   .   .   .
>
> Peace, perfect peace, with sorrows surging round?
> On Jesus' bosom naught but calm is found.
>
> .   .   .   .
>
> Peace, perfect peace, our future all unknown?
> Jesus we know, and He is on the throne."

Ready were these two saintly spirits for death for the sake of Christ, which they momentarily expected. But, to their surprise, no order was given. The executioner shouldered his axe. Mr. and Mrs. Porteous were released, and permitted to return to their headquarters in Shanghai. And later, back in their homeland, they were enabled to relate the story of their singing faith in the hour of expected death.

CHAPTER VIII

SORROW AND SONG

" No friend like music when the heart is broken,
To mend its wings and give it flight again;
No friend like music, breaking chains and bars
To let the soul march with the quiet stars! "
—Daniel Whitehead Hickey in
" The New York Times."

Many bereavements came into the life of Charlotte Elliot,
and she was also a lifelong invalid, but her spirit was " sweetly
resigned." In fact, when facing her great sorrows, she was accustomed to sing some verses from one of her own comforting
hymns:

" What though in lonely grief I sigh
For friends beloved, no longer nigh,
Submissive still would I reply,
' Thy will be done! '

" If Thou should'st call me to resign
What most I prize, it ne'er was mine:
I only yield Thee what is Thine;
' Thy will be done! '

.   .   .   .   .

" Renew my will from day to day,
Blend it with Thine, and take away
All that now makes it hard to say,
' Thy will be done! ' "

112

" A bit of praise is one of the best ways of dispelling a dark mood. I knew a man who lost his speech during the war. It was a mild case of shell-shock. One Sunday evening he was at a religious service and the company broke into the words of the 100th Psalm. Forgetting his weakness, he made the effort and found that his bonds were loosed. Speech had come back. A song of praise in the prison of gloom or depression can open the prison doors."—*The Rev. James Reid, D.D., in " The British Weekly."*

Singing After the Mining Disaster

A fresh tribute to the living and sustaining power of the beloved hymn of Charles Wesley:

> " Jesus, Lover of my soul,
>   Let me to Thy bosom fly,"

came from across the Atlantic in December, 1910. A colliery accident occurred, which was regarded as the worst which had happened in England in forty-five years. There was an explosion in the Pretoria Pit, near Bolton, and about 320 men lost their lives. The accident occurred early in the morning, and during the day immense crowds of people assembled on an embankment overlooking the shaft, while rescue teams were at work.

Late on that sad December afternoon the Bishop of Manchester held a service for the bereaved, which the correspondent of *The Times* thus described:

" The light was growing dim, and the watchers were gradually losing the faint hope with which they had buoyed themselves up for so many hours, when the Bishop and a local clergyman stepped into the midst of them and asked them to sing, ' Jesus, Lover of My Soul.' It was a moment of such intense solemnity as a man feels but once in a lifetime, and the quivering voices with which the women answered his request revealed the extent of their grief and the measure of their suffering."

Pathetic in the extreme was the picture of those wives, children, mothers and friends, hoping against hope, with their breaking hearts and their tear-dimmed eyes, endeavoring to sing:

" Other refuge have I none;
    Hangs my helpless soul on Thee;
Leave, ah! leave me not alone,
    Still support and comfort me:
All my trust on Thee is stayed,
    All my help from Thee I bring;
Cover my defenseless head
    With the shadow of Thy wing."

Many are the stories which have gathered around this hymn, which is commonly considered to be the masterpiece of Charles Wesley, and which is by many regarded as " the finest heart hymn in the English language." No nobler mission is the high privilege of man than to give strength and courage to the living, and comfort and hope to the dying. This Charles Wesley has been doing during the many years in which saints and sinners have sung, " Jesus, Lover of My Soul."

"Two lines of this hymn," said Dr. Theodore L. Cuyler, one of Brooklyn's beloved ministers during the latter part of the nineteenth century, " have been breathed frequently and often out of bleeding hearts. When we were once in the valley of death-shade, with one beautiful child in the new-made grave and the other threatened with fatal disease, there was no prayer that we said oftener than this:

" ' Leave, ah! leave me not alone,
    Still support and comfort me.' "

The Day After Calvin Coolidge's Funeral

Ex-President Calvin Coolidge was buried on Saturday, January 7, 1933, following his sudden death. The next

morning Mrs. Coolidge was in the family pew at the
Edwards Congregational Church, Northampton, Massachusetts. This was where she and Mr. Coolidge attended
church regularly when they were at their family home.
Now her distinguished husband was removed from her;
but she was accompanied by her son, John, as well as by
a friend or two. The opening hymn selected for the service that morning was the familiar one:

> " Come, Thou almighty King,
> Help us Thy name to sing,
> Help us to praise! "

The newspapers told the American people the next day
that Mrs. Coolidge followed her usual habit of joining
with the congregation in singing the hymns. It was a
brave and beautiful thing to do on such an occasion.
The sorrow in her heart did not prevent her from raising
her voice in praiseful song; and one can easily imagine
that she found comfort and strength as she joined in this
hymn of worship.

The compilers of the " Inter-Church Hymnal," in their
investigations, found that this hymn is sung more frequently than any other at services of worship in the
United States, and therefore they placed it first in that
hymnal. Though attributed very often to Charles Wesley,
yet the well-informed writers consider it to be anonymous.
But, as Nutter and Tillett said: " It is an ideal hymn for
the beginning of a great Christian hymnal, as well as for
the opening of public worship."

Amid the sorrow of her spirit, the former " First Lady
of the Land " sang her plea for divine help in the words:

> " Come, Holy Comforter."

" Peace, Perfect Peace! "

Queen Mary selected as the hymn to be sung at the
memorial service at Sandringham for King George V a
song of hope, comfort and assurance. The hymn chosen
for the occasion was one which had been a favorite with
the King's grandmother, Queen Victoria, and it was sung
in her chamber when she was on her deathbed. It was
the lovely hymn of Bishop E. H. Bickersteth:

> " Peace, perfect peace, in this dark world of sin?
> The blood of Jesus whispers peace within."

The later stanzas bring a message of gracious consola-
tion to anxious, sorrowing spirits:

> " Peace, perfect peace, with sorrows surging round?
> On Jesus' bosom naught but calm is found.

> " Peace, perfect peace, with loved ones far away?
> In Jesus' keeping we are safe and they."

In the village church at Sandringham, where the royal
family were accustomed to worship with their neighbors,
and where gamekeepers and others employed on the
King's estate stood guard over his body as it lay in state
before being removed to London, and later to Windsor
for burial, this hymn was sung. Newspapers reported,
however, that the Queen who made this choice of a hymn
" was too affected to join in the singing."

This hymn is peculiar in the fact that it presents a series
of direct questions in the first line, and then proceeds to
give positive and appropriate answers, with reasons for
the same, in the second line. This is " a peculiarity ex-
quisitely rendered by the music to which it is commonly

sung," remarks Dr. Charles S. Robinson; "the first strain bearing the plaintive and wistful tone of the questioner, and the following strain replying with a bright and vigorous promise from the words of our Saviour."

This hymn comes "very near 'Lead, Kindly Light,' in combining piety and poetry in the highest proportion" in the opinion of Richard le Gallienne, who bore this personal testimony: "It would be difficult to name any other hymn so filled with the sense of man's security as this, which tranquillizes me at certain moments to a remarkable degree."

Canadian Mother Sustained After Losing Three Sons

Living in a Canadian community in 1914 were a family that included five sons. One day that year they read a special edition of a newspaper stating that Canada would have to send 500,000 men to the war which had just been declared. Some of the boys in that home had reached military age, the oldest being twenty-two. Before the close of the next year three of the boys had gone into uniform.

One of these boys was in the third battle of Ypres, June, 1916. Less than twenty of his company came out, though they went in a full number. He wrote his mother stating that though bullets rained thick and fast around him, yet he remained unharmed. Later, however, on a September day, he fell at the battle of Courcelette—shot through the heart. The mother was just preparing to write him a long letter when she received the terse message, "Killed in action." Later came a letter from the youth which was written the day before the battle. One of his comrades crept out into No Man's Land where the body lay, took from his pocket the New Testament which he always carried, and sent it back to the family.

April 9, 1917, the oldest son fell at Vimy Ridge.

Still there was hope that the third boy would return home. But on September 17, 1918, less than two months before the armistice was signed, this lad was also instantly killed while giving aid to the wounded.

A few years later the mother published the story of those years of anguish and loss.* Said she: "There was the great sorrow which would have crushed, but did not because of the consciousness of the Master's presence and upholding power, and the words that gave me most comfort then were those of one of Wesley's hymns."

The hymn of this bereaved Canadian mother begins:

> "Peace, doubting heart! my God's I am;
>   Who formed me man, forbids my fear."

In "The Methodist Hymn Book," London, it is placed under the heading of "The Christian Life," and the division, "Trustfulness and Peace." This mother, out of her own experience, also quoted the second stanza:

> "When, passing through the watery deep,
>   I ask in faith His promised aid,
> The waves an awful distance keep,
>   And shrink from my devoted head;
> Fearless their violence I dare;
> They cannot harm, for God is there."

This hymn, quoted by the Canadian mother, was inspired by one of the great passages of Isaiah (43: 1, 2): "Fear not: for I have redeemed thee, I have called thee by thy name; thou art mine. When thou passest through

* *The Sunday School Times*, May 24, 1934.

the waters, I will be with thee; and through the rivers, they shall not overflow thee."

Said that good mother, in closing her story: " There are times when I look downwards to the three graves somewhere in France. . . . Then I remember that it cannot be long before I shall go to them . . . and I find that the joy of the Lord is my strength."

> " When darkness intercepts the skies
> And sorrow's waves around me roll,
>
> .   .   .   .   .
>
> My soul a sudden calm shall feel,
> And hear a whisper: Peace; be still! "

Midnight Music at a Railroad Station

> " Nearer, my God, to Thee,
> Nearer to Thee!
> E'en though it be a cross
> That raiseth me;
> Still all my song shall be,
> Nearer, my God, to Thee,
> Nearer to Thee! "

The closing years of the nineteenth century found thousands of persons, on both sides of the Atlantic, reading " Beside the Bonnie Brier Bush." The author, Dr. John Watson ("Ian Maclaren"), was born and educated in Scotland; exercised a long ministry at Sefton Park Church, Liverpool, England; and died in America.

This distinguished preacher and writer came to the United States for the purpose of lecturing and preaching. He went to Mount Pleasant, Iowa, to deliver some lectures at Iowa Wesleyan University, and there he died. He was taken back to Liverpool for burial. There they placed on his coffin, by his own request, his Master of Arts hood, and " a simple cross of white flowers.".

Mrs. Watson left Mount Pleasant on a midnight train for New York, as she accompanied the body of her husband on his last trip and voyage. With her, also, was a friend. A large body of students from the university, and also members of the faculty, gathered at the station to express their sympathy for the one whose husband had been taken from her while in a foreign land. Dr. William R. Nicoll, the biographer of Dr. Watson, said:

" During the short time preceding the arrival of the train the old college bell tolled off the fifty-seven years of Watson's life. Just before the train arrived and the party were on the platform to await its drawing into the station, there rang out sweetly and comfortingly on the still night air the strains of the hymn:

" ' Nearer, my God, to Thee.' "

Thus did America voice its last tribute to the distinguished visitor with a hymn sung by the assembled company.

Salvation Army Sang the Doxology

Three men were exploring an old gold mine at Moose River, Nova Scotia, in April, 1936, and when they were on the 141-foot level the old shaft, their entrance and exit, collapsed. The mine had been abandoned in 1921, and two men from Toronto, Dr. D. E. Robertson, a physician, and Herman R. Magill, a lawyer, had bought the rights. They decided to make a tour of their property to ascertain what was needed to restore it to working condition. With them they took a guide, Charles A. Scadding. The lowest level was 360 feet, so they were far from the bottom of the mine when the accident occurred.

Newspapers carried the news over the United States and Canada. One of the news reports gave this description: "Expert miners, physicians and police were rushed to the spot by the Nova Scotia government; the Minister of Health and the Premier went to Moose River; relatives of the entombed men, reporters, photographers and other spectators crowded the village. . . ."

Rescue workers by the score relieved each other all through the day and night. They dared not use explosives, and so the work was painfully slow. A pipe was forced through, that food might be provided, and a telephone line was established through the pipe. But water began to rise around the men, and thus communication became more difficult.

Four Salvation Army workers from Halifax soon reached the scene of disaster and served coffee, chocolate and fruit to the rescue workers during the period which was tense with anxiety. They also gave the people courage by their spiritual ministry.

Ten days passed before the workers, lifting away some big rocks, were able to enter the tunnel. The physician and the guide were alive. But Mr. Magill, unable to endure the prolonged cold and moisture, had died three days before the rescuers came.

When the two living men, and the one who had died, were brought to the surface and cared for, the ministry of the representatives of the Salvation Army assumed a different form. Now they led the people in a hymn sing, but first of all they expressed their gratitude in the lines of the old doxology. The Associated Press summed up the situation by saying:

"Humble in the face of death, but thankful that two lives had been saved, the miners who succeeded in the rescue, the officials who directed their work, and the spectators who were drawn to the isolated settlement by the international anxiety attending the entombment, joined in singing:

"'Praise God from Whom All Blessings Flow.'"

Two lives had been preserved for ten days in the dark and dampness of the mines, and grateful hearts sang, amid their sorrow for the one life which had been taken:

> "Praise God from Whom all blessings flow,
> Praise Him, all creatures here below;
> Praise Him above, ye heavenly host;
> Praise Father, Son, and Holy Ghost."

CHAPTER IX

CHRISTMAS CAROLS

" And suddenly there was with the angel a multitude of the heavenly host praising God, and saying:

" Glory to God in the highest,
And on earth peace among men in whom he is well pleased."

(Luke 2: 13, 14, R. V.)

" There is no music in the world that can compare with our Christmas music. There is no music that finds its way into the heart of the world's suffering, the world's questioning and the world's peace, like this Christian music."—*Professor William T. Hocking, of Harvard University, when speaking at Drew University on " Christianity and the Non-Christian Religions."*

" How I, like countless others, love Christmas! The secrets, the excitement, the spirit of added cheeriness on every side, and the fun of it all mean so much to me. . . .

" When my roomful of little Portuguese first and second graders softly sing ' Silent Night ' it seems to tell me way down deep inside that Christmas Time is truly here."—*Miss Helen Lawrence Crocker, Newport, R. I., in a communication to " The New York Times," December, 1938.*

" Princeton and Bryn Mawr College choirs united at Christmastide in a full rendition of Handel's ' Messiah.' As I listened to those mighty choruses from Scripture, which seemed to pound themselves into one's innermost being, I thought less about the music itself than about the singers, those scores of fine, talented young men and women who performed so skilfully and lustily.

" For the music was working a permanent effect upon their lives. No matter where they go or what they become, these triumphant Scriptural passages will remain in their memory until they die.

" In serving others, they more greatly served themselves."
—William T. Ellis in " The Christian Herald."

Gridiron Club Sang a Christmas Song

" Away in a manger, no crib for a bed,
The little Lord Jesus laid down His sweet head.
The stars in the sky looked down where He lay,
The little Lord Jesus asleep on the hay."

More than five hundred newspaper men and their guests, including President Franklin D. Roosevelt, attended the Winter dinner of the Gridiron Club in Washington, D. C., on December 17, 1938, and one feature made the gathering historic. The newspaper men had their evening of fun as they rendered their program. Newspapers reported the events of the evening in detail, and related the surprise features. *The New York Times* the next day closed its special article with the words:

" The lights were dimmed and there was silence for a moment, and the group was reminded of the approach of Christmas. The Gridiron Club did something it never had done before. It ended its dinner with a hymn:

" ' Away in a manger, no crib for a bed,
The little Lord Jesus laid down His sweet head.' "

So that body of newspaper men made history that night when they sang their Christmas song. Those men, in the closest contact with daily life, made a beautiful selection for the occasion. Lovely lines, tender and simple, rich in their human appeal, are these—

" The cattle are lowing, the Baby awakes,
But little Lord Jesus, no crying He makes.
I love Thee, Lord Jesus, look down from the sky,
And stay by my cradle till morning is nigh."

The authorship of this hymn is regarded as uncertain, though it has most often been credited to Martin Luther. The style, however, is unlike that of Luther's other hymns. Yet Covert and Laufer ("Handbook to the Hymnal," Presbyterian) say that: "It has not been considered an incongruity to ascribe to him this tender and lovely carol that for centuries, in the several tongues of many lands, has been the lullaby sung over the beds of countless children."

Modern hymnals are commonly including this in their collection. Thus it is found in "The Hymnary" of the United Church of Canada and also in "The New Canadian Hymnal"; likewise it is found in such recent books as "The Hymnal" (Presbyterian), "The Methodist Hymnal," and also "The Methodist Hymn Book" (London).

Dr. Robert Guy McCutchan in "Our Hymnody" tells us that the third stanza was written by Dr. John T. McFarland at the request of Bishop William F. Anderson in the first decade of the present century. After the latter had asked Dr. McFarland to write another stanza to go with the first and the second, he went to his office and returned in about an hour with the words:

> "Be near me, Lord Jesus, I ask Thee to stay
> Close by me forever, and love me, I pray.
> Bless all the dear children in Thy tender care,
> And fit us for heaven to live with Thee there."

This carol is mostly sung to the tune of "Cradle Song," composed by William J. Kirkpatrick, who, though a business man in Pennsylvania, devoted much time to sacred music.

This Christmas song, which the newspaper men sang in

the nation's capital at Christmastide, has also " been the message to unnumbered little children, by which they have learned to know and love ' the little Lord Jesus.' "

Christmas Recaptured

" O little town of Bethlehem,
　　How still we see thee lie!
Above thy deep and dreamless sleep
　　The silent stars go by;
Yet in thy dark streets shineth
　　The everlasting Light;
The hopes and fears of all the years
　　Are met in thee tonight."

Christmas is a mood and not merely a day, we are sometimes reminded. Therefore if the mood be lost, the day loses its significance. The story of the woman who lost Christmas and then found it again has been related by herself. The letter telling how she found the Christmas she once had lost reached *The New York Times* three days after Christmas, 1933, when she sent a thank-offering for the " Hundred Neediest Cases." Said the writer:

" When I was a child I had an unshakable belief in humanity and God and Christmas—and a soul sensitive to beauty. Growing up did cruel things to my beautiful belief, and for the past few years Christmas has meant nothing to me much more than a chance to celebrate. To be sophisticated one must be skeptical; to betray the slightest hint of spiritual emotion would quickly finish one in the rôle of a blasé modern. So it is a long time since I've seen anything in Christmas beyond the glitter of the tinselled tree. . . . Then, one night last week I found the vision of beauty again in the face of a schoolboy singing ' Little Town of Bethlehem.'

" It is because of my joy at having finally recaptured the true mood of Christmas, and thereby the meaning of all life, that I offer my contribution to the Neediest. I'm sorry it's so paltry—but so much had previously been spent for tinsel.

" Mary."

Thus more than sixty years after Bishop Phillips Brooks wrote his beautiful Christmas carol in Philadelphia, the message of the song enabled a woman in New York to recapture the true mood of Christmas. A gift of love for the needy expressed, in part, her gratitude. This happened when she heard a schoolboy singing the lovely words of one of America's saints.

> " How silently, how silently
>   The wondrous gift is given!
> So God imparts to human hearts
>   The blessings of His heaven.
> No ear may hear His coming,
>   But in this world of sin,
> Where meek souls will receive Him still,
>   The dear Christ enters in."

Kiwanians Aid Salvation Army at Christmas

Christmas Day would come within less than a week, and the members of the Kiwanis Club in the North Country city of Watertown, New York, learned that the kettles of the Salvation Army needed to be filled more rapidly if every needy family in the city were to be supplied with a well-filled basket of food. What could these busy business and professional men do to help, in addition to their personal gifts? They could give something of themselves for an hour or two, they decided. Soon they got into

action. So during the rush period little groups went forth
to their assignments.

Big bells, vigorously rung, attracted attention, while
the old-time sleigh bells, now so rarely heard, were jin-
gling their cheery music. The day was mild, and there was
just enough snow to suggest Christmas. Hence the side-
walks were crowded. But the folks looked with unbeliev-
ing eyes when they saw doctor, lawyer, manufacturer, and
others ringing their bells in front of the Salvation Army
kettles in the public Square. Furthermore, the men had so
arranged themselves that the people had to pass near
these kettles. They evidently knew the psychology of sales-
manship; and so they played Santa Claus, without the
whiskers and the red garments.

A company of selected singers, also Kiwanians, met
their assignment by moving from one kettle to another.
Standing near a kettle they rendered the Christmas music
which everybody knows and loves. A minister was in this
group, and there was a young man who accompanied the
singers with his accordion.

Clerks and customers rushed from stores as they heard
the chorus singing the echoing words of Isaac Watts to
the thrilling tune of " Antioch ":

> " Joy to the world! the Lord is come:
>   Let earth receive her King:
>   Let every heart prepare Him room,
>   And heaven and nature sing."

Then they eagerly dropped their money in the kettle. Office employees on some of the upper floors raised their
windows to listen, and then tossed down coins which the
Kiwanians gathered up for the Salvation Army fund.

" Silent Night " in the Congo

Following a heavy storm, some missionaries were unable to cross a river for the purpose of reaching one of their stations for an early service on Christmas morning. They managed, however, to find a hotel. Unexpected guests, no arrangements had been made for them; but they were given a cup of tea and a *straw bed*. With such a bed on Christmas Eve, the meaning of Christmas was deeply impressed upon them. Julia Lake Kellersberger, who relates the incident in " Congo Crosses," * says:

" Suddenly we heard exquisite music as of angels' voices singing, ' Glory to God in the Highest and on Earth Peace, Good-will to men.' . . . We strained our ears to listen. It was just three o'clock and still dark and cold. Nearer and nearer, deeper and richer were the voices singing:

> " ' Silent night, holy night,
> All is calm, all is bright,'

in the beautiful native tongue. It was a group of joyous African Christians, awakening the dawn with their Christmas music. No white missionary was there to lead them. It was a spontaneous expression of their gratitude to God for the birth of His Son."

Thus, as the writer intimated, God had used the Africans, and the song which they sang, to teach the missionaries themselves the deeper meaning of Christmas.

* Published by the Central Committee on the United Study of Foreign Missions.

Christmas Carol and Christmas Prayer

" It came upon the midnight clear,
That glorious song of old,
From angels bending near the earth,
To touch their harps of gold."

Vividly descriptive is the story of " our carol singing party " in " The Midnight Clear " by H. L. Gee, an English writer.* The author tells of a group, somewhere in England, who, on Christmas Eve, representing their church, went out to sing carols. The night, cold, damp, foggy, was unpleasant. But over roads, though lanes, and across muddy fields, the company of musicians wended their way to convey Christmas cheer to the aged, the sick, and the lonely. " There were nine countrymen with musical instruments, and fifteen singers, eight men and seven girls—most of them young, though Harry Dodds, who sang tenor, was turned sixty, and Joe Winthrope, who led off every tune, was over seventy." They rendered, as far as they knew the preferences of families or individuals, the carols the individuals or families most loved.

The musicians went up " the wettest muddiest lane in England's green and pleasant land," and sang their loudest for one " queer old chap who lived alone." Quite overcome, he whispered his thanks in the words, " God bless ye." Hot coffee, sandwiches, mince pies and hot chestnuts were among the things they were served to eat and drink. There were other gifts also—and appreciation always. One of the company said to the visiting member accompanying them, " You might think us fellows was doing this here for other folks. Don't you believe it. We does it

* *The Methodist Recorder.*

to put Christmas in our *own* hearts, you see. It wouldn't be Christmas for *us* if we didn't make it for somebody else."

Last of all the group left the lane, made their way across some fields, and were welcomed into a farmhouse. There they were shown into a huge parlor in one corner of which was a four-poster bed, and in the bed there was a white-haired woman—the farmer's wife. " She lay there like a queen, propped up with pillows, a shawl about her shoulders." She smiled as the family all gathered in the bedroom, for she had been looking forward to this moment all the year.

" I don't know whether you have ever heard a brass band in a parlor or not," said the one who narrated the incident, " but if you have not you have missed a treat— providing only the players know how to modulate their tones." Again some of the familiar carols were rendered. Then they closed with:

> " It came upon the midnight clear,
> That glorious song of old."

Then, though no signal was given, the woman in the bed began to pray, as the entire company bowed their heads. This was the prayer:

" Lord Jesus, dear Lord Jesus, the fields are dark, the night is cold, the hour is late. Blessed Lord, there's light and warmth within this house and the door is open wide. Come in, Lord Jesus, come. Abide with us forever. Rest here and be at home. Little Jesus, come."

" Amen," the others softly said.

It was the prayer of one who had been confined to her bed for nearly thirty years. Said one to the visitor, " She's a saint of God, you can see it in her face."

The clock in the church tower, a mile away, was striking twelve, and the visitor reverently whispered, " It came upon the midnight clear."

This is " one of the first of the carol-like hymns that seem to have sprung from American poets." The author, Edmund Hamilton Sears, D.D., was born in Sandisfield, Massachusetts, April 16, 1810, and graduated from Union College and the Divinity School of Harvard University. The hymn first appeared in the *Christian Register,* Boston, December, 1850. The editor, the Rev. Dr. Morrison, was delighted with this composition, and afterward he wrote: " I always feel that, however poor my Christmas sermon may be, the reading and singing of this hymn are enough to make up for all deficiencies."

Heard " Silent Night " Sung by Schumann-Heink

" Oh, that is such a lovely song! " exclaimed Schumann-Heink as she spoke of " Stille Nacht " (" Silent Night, Holy Night "). Mary Lawton, in relating the story of the life of this beloved singer, tells us that she " had a great love for the simple songs which reach the hearts of people everywhere." Naturally, being a German by birth, she had a peculiar fondness for this hymn which brings the very spirit of Christmas into the hearts of the people of all ages.

" I sang this song once, and my records went even to South America," said the singer. This was before the days of radio. Letters came to her, she said, from the nurses in a hospital telling her how they put that record on a phonograph on Christmas Eve. The message said that they all cried—" nurses and doctors, as well as the sick ones." They all united in thanking the singer for this message in song. "That touched me very much," Schumann-Heink confessed as she related the incident.

The incident was a tribute to the famous singer, to the author of the hymn, and to the composer of the tune.

> " Silent night, holy night,
> Wondrous Star, lend thy light;
> With the angels let us sing,
> Alleluia to our King;
> Christ the Saviour is born."

Appropriate was it that " Silent Night " should be sung at the funeral of this beloved singer, though it was a November day rather than one in December when she was buried. During the World War she endeared herself by her readiness to sing for those who were giving themselves for her adopted country. Said the Associated Press in a note from San Diego, California, on the day of her burial, after she died at the age of seventy-five:

" Men who fought in the trenches, mothers who lost their sons in battle, and hundreds of others who loved Mme. Ernestine Schumann-Heink wept openly today as they heard the soft strains of her favorite song in the chapel where her body lay in a flower-draped casket.

" Outside were more hundreds."

A description of the service followed, and then:

" The clear bugle notes of Taps filled the chapel.

" Soft strains of ' Silent Night, Holy Night '—from the harp and 'cello followed."

This was what she would have desired. The Christmas song which she so dearly loved and so devoutly sang in life was the final selection played by the musicians when she slept " in heavenly peace."

CHAPTER X

HEARD AT GETHSEMANE
AND CALVARY

" Gethsemane can I forget,
    Or there Thy conflict see,
Thine agony and bloody sweat,
    And not remember Thee?

" When to the cross I turn mine eyes,
    And rest on Calvary,
O Lamb of God, my Sacrifice,
    I must remember Thee! "

" Standing on the summit of the green hill far away, outside the city wall, I sang the fine old gospel hymn:

" ' On Calvary's brow my Saviour died.' "
—" *My Life and the Story of the Gospel Hymns,*"
by Ira D. Sankey (Harper & Brothers), p. 89.

" Perhaps the greatest significance of any song was when Jesus sang at the Last Supper. With persecution behind and suffering in the offing, Jesus joined with His disciples in singing a hymn. Then He went out to Gethsemane to pray.

" It would be thrilling to know just what song it was that Christ did sing. But the significance of the incident is that He was able, though practically on His way to His death, to sing at all. But He did sing, and that at one of the most difficult moments of His life."—*The War Cry.*

" It is my opinion that few of the classic pieces in the hymnody of the Christian Church have more perfectly voiced the sense of the mystery of the redeeming love than has this one tremendous stanza:

> " ' But none of the ransomed ever knew
>   How deep were the waters crossed,
>   Nor how dark was the night that the Lord passed through
>   Ere He found His sheep that was lost.'

That joy in the thought of an almost unbelievable deliverance is at the center of Christian experience."—*The Rev. J. V. Moldenhawer, D.D., in " The Church Tower."*

Julia Ward Howe in Gethsemane

The famous Julia Ward Howe, accompanied by her daughter, Mrs. Maude Howe Elliott, once visited the Garden of Gethsemane. The daughter recorded the fact that on this occasion her mother " was more silent than usual." Evidently she was in a deeply meditative mood.

" Would you mind if I sang a hymn? " the older woman asked. She then " raised her sweet voice," and with a beautiful sense of appropriateness began to sing the hymn of James Montgomery:

" Go to dark Gethsemane,
　　Ye that feel the tempter's power;
　Your Redeemer's conflict see,
　　Watch with Him one bitter hour;
　Turn not from His griefs away,
　　Learn of Jesus Christ to pray."

Though some American hymnals have omitted this strikingly descriptive hymn, yet it is retained in " The Hymnal " of the Episcopal Church (published in 1916), and is also given a place in " The Hymnary " (of the United Church of Canada).

Mrs. Howe and her daughter lingered under " the garden's immemorial olives and cedars," after Mrs. Howe had sung her hymn. The guide presented Mrs. Howe with a handful of flowers. Many years afterward the daughter found them in an envelope marked " Gethsemane."

The author headed this hymn thus, " Christ Our Example in Suffering." The Rev. John Telford gives an incident from the Rev. James King relative to a visit which he made to the world's most historic garden. The company sat down on a rock overlooking the garden. " The moon was still bright, and the venerable olive-trees were casting dark shadows across the sacred ground. No human voice was heard, and the stillness was only broken by the occasional barking of dogs in the city. We read, by the light, passages bearing on the agony, and James Montgomery's solemn hymn, ' Go to Dark Gethsemane.' "

Midnight Song on Mount Olivet

During the latter part of the nineteenth century Mr. George C. Stebbins, an American leader of evangelistic music and the composer of many tunes, made an extensive trip to various Eastern countries. While in Palestine he and several friends, from both the United States and England, visited " the places made forever sacred by the footsteps of our Lord." But the experience which impressed him most was a visit to the Mount of Olives.

One moonlight night a small company of friends took lanterns—for there were then no street lights—and passed through the gates of the city of Jerusalem into the Garden of Gethsemane. Then, climbing the slopes of the Mount of Olives, they sat down to view the city from that mountainside. Many others joined them, and they thus visualized the Christ and the company that followed Him. Said Mr. Stebbins in his " Reminiscences ": " While our thoughts were recalling that saddest of all the world's events, one of the party began singing a hymn in which we all joined with a sense of reality most solemn and impressive."

One can almost imagine that company of American and English visitors, with the distinguished composer and song leader as one of their number, as they united in singing:

" 'Tis midnight; and on Olive's brow
　　The star is dimmed that lately shone:
　'Tis midnight; in the garden now
　　The suffering Saviour prays alone."

The author of this beautiful hymn, William B. Tappan, was born in Beverly, Massachusetts, October 29, 1794. He became a school teacher in New Jersey, and later he entered the service of the American Sunday School Union. " His artistic ability as a writer was one of his strongest characteristics." But though he published several volumes of poetry, yet he lives through this hymn, " 'Tis Midnight," which Mr. Stebbins and his group sang while they were assembled on that distant night on Mount Olivet.

Musician Sang His Tune on Calvary

" There is a green hill far away,
　　Without a city wall,
　Where the dear Lord was crucified
　　Who died to save us all.

. . . . . .

" He died that we might be forgiven,
　　He died to make us good,
　That we might go at last to heaven,
　　Saved by His precious blood."

This hymn was written at the bedside of a sick child. After she recovered she always claimed the hymn as her own. Its author wrote about four hundred hymns and poems for children, including the following:

" Once in royal David's city
　　Stood a lowly cattle shed,
　Where a mother laid her Baby

In a manger for His bed:
Mary was that mother mild,
Jesus Christ her little Child."

It was in 1848 that Mrs. Cecil Frances Alexander, who was but twenty-five years of age, published her " Hymns for Little Children." The volume " endeared her to many hearts." One writer affirms that " all her pieces are characterized by a winning simplicity." The song of the " Green Hill " has won wide popularity both among children and older people. Its use is twofold, and may be found in our hymnals either among the group for children, or under hymns which relate to the cross of Christ. It is " one of the finest for children and one of the really great hymns on the atonement." The writer of the hymn became the wife of the Rev. William Alexander, who later served as Bishop of Derry, Ireland.

Though other tunes are used in various hymnals, yet the one which is associated with the hymn when it is used by children is " Green Hill," which was composed by one of America's beloved musicians—George C. Stebbins. They love to sing the chorus to the music of Mr. Stebbins:

" Oh, dearly, dearly has He loved,
And we must love Him too;
And trust in His redeeming blood,
And try His works to do."

Mr. Sankey once wrote to Mr. Stebbins concerning this hymn, saying, " While holding meetings with Mr. Moody at Cardiff, Wales, in 1883, I visited the ruins of Tintern Abbey with Professor (Henry) Drummond, and sang this hymn, which Mr. Drummond said was one of the finest in the English language."

Several years after Mr. Stebbins composed his appealing tune, he had a unique experience with the same. He records it very briefly and simply, but one can easily imagine that it gave him untold happiness. Said he concerning the hymn:

" I sang it on the ' Green Hill,' believed to be Calvary, outside the walls of Jerusalem."

The beautiful combination of words and music has been given the world by the wife of an Irish bishop and one of America's composers.

William Booth on Mount Calvary

The flag of the Salvation Army was unfurled by General William Booth, founder of the Salvation Army, after he had climbed Mount Calvary under a hot sun. The General made this visit in March, 1905, during a trip to the Holy Land. With characteristic loyalty to Christ and His cross, and revealing his spirit of consecration, he quoted, as he displayed the flag, the words:

> " Were the whole realm of nature mine,
>   That were an offering far too small;
>   Love so amazing, so divine,
>   Demands my soul, my life, my all."

Following his habit of frequently kneeling in prayer, the venerable General knelt down on the historic and sacred soil of Calvary and prayed. Then, gathering a few flowers, we went and laid them on the traditional tomb of Christ.

The lines General Booth quoted on that day came from the cherished hymn of Isaac Watts:

" When I survey the wondrous cross,
    On which the Prince of Glory died,
    My richest gain I count but loss,
    And pour contempt on all my pride."

This has always been regarded as one of the choicest hymns of the Christian Church. Writing in 1897, W. T. Stead said: " This is one of the four hymns which stand at the head of all hymns in the English language." The spirit of devotion in a congregation is always deepened by the singing of this hymn. How appropriate, therefore, that it should have been quoted by such a sacrificial follower of Christ on Calvary's hill!

Aged and blind, William Booth entered into life eternal on October 20, 1912, and above him as he closed his eyes in death was the flag which he had taken around the world and unfurled on Calvary. During his entire life he had been true to the lines which he quoted on that March day seven years earlier at the place where his Lord had been crucified.

Easter Morning on the Mount of Olives

" Thine be the glory, risen, conquering Son,
    Endless is the victory Thou o'er death hast won;
    Angels in bright raiment rolled the stone away,
    Kept the folded grave-clothes, where Thy body lay."

The Jerusalem Missionary Conference, " a kind of miniature Universal Church, gathered from East and West and South and North," met in the city of Jerusalem in the spring of 1928. The 240 representatives spoke sixty different tongues. This gathering met on the Mount of

Olives on Easter morning, and sang the Easter hymn here indicated. Mr. E. S. Lamplough, an Englishman devoted to music, was present, and afterward indicated that the thrill experienced was something which could never be expressed in words. One can almost imagine the assembly, coming from various parts of the world, as they sang on that eventful morning:

> " Lo! Jesus meets us, risen from the tomb;
> Lovingly He greets us, scatters fear and gloom;
> Let the Church with gladness, hymns of triumph sing,
> For her Lord now liveth, death hath lost its sting."

This hymn appears in " The Methodist Hymn Book," London, and was written in 1904 by Edmond Louis Burdy, a pastor at Vevey, Switzerland. The translation was made by the Rev. Birch Hoyle, a Baptist minister, for the English Y. M. C. A., and appeared in *The Red Triangle,* of which he was the editor. The tune used for the hymn is " Maccabæus " from Handel's " Judas Maccabæus." Triumphant is the refrain of this Easter hymn:

> " Thine be the glory, risen, conquering Son,
> Endless is the victory Thou o'er death hast won."

CHAPTER XI

THE WONDROUS CROSS

" Above the hills of time the cross is gleaming,
  Fair as the sun when night has turned to day;
  And from it love's pure light is richly streaming,
  To cleanse the heart and banish sin away."

—Thomas Tiplady.

A young man preparing for the ministry attended a service in City Temple, London, on an October evening in 1899, for the purpose of hearing Dr. Joseph Parker. He sat with other theological students in the pulpit immediately behind the preacher. The memory of that service was so persistent that thirty-eight years afterward the Rev. A. Cunningham-Burley thus described the occasion, when, after singing the General Confession, the time for prayer was reached: " The preacher stood quite motionless with closed eyes. Presently Parker moved before beginning to pray. There was a strange kneading of the thumbs over the clasped hands, and then with a depth of feeling trembling in the old man's voice he managed to say:

" ' In my hands no price I bring,
  Simply to *Thy Cross* I cling.' Amen.

" It would be impossible to describe the effect of these simple words upon the congregation. We could manage to listen to the sermon that followed without a tear, but found it quite impossible to do so to that soul-moving invocation."*—The Christian World.*

" Upon that cross of Jesus
  Mine eye at times can see
  The very dying form of One
  Who suffered there for me."

—Elizabeth C. Clephane.

144

" We are nowadays hearing less frequently than we used to that sterling baritone, Oscar Seagle. But in the days when he gave his concerts often, it was almost a custom with him to sing before he finished his program that magnificent thriller of evangelistic days:

" ' There were ninety and nine that safely lay
In the shelter of the fold,
But one was out on the hills away,
Far off from the gates of gold.'

His audiences were always enthralled. . . . The tumult of pain and fear, of rescue and triumph in that singing was something indescribable."—*The Rev. J. V. Moldenhawer, D.D., in " The Church Tower."*

" Jesus Christ, the Crucified "

> " Ask ye what great thing I know
> That delights and stirs me so?
> What the high reward I win?
> Whose the name I glory in?
> Jesus Christ the Crucified."

Three hundred ministers made a peaceful invasion of West Point late in the year of 1935. They were located in the Thayer Hotel, and used the spacious assembly room for the services during their period of " retreat." There, amid rugged mountain scenery, surrounded by the glowing glory of the trees in their resplendent autumn beauty, and with the gently flowing Hudson River in sight, they spent three days in meditation and song.

One of the evening speakers was the Rev. J. V. Moldenhawer, D.D., minister of the First Presbyterian Church, New York City. Toward the close of the address, Dr. Moldenhawer quoted the opening lines of the hymn of Dr. Isaac Watts:

> " When I survey the wondrous cross
> On which the Prince of Glory died."

Fresh emphasis was given the word *" survey."* The speaker indicated that we were not merely to glance at the cross in a casual, momentary fashion. But we were to *survey* it—unhurriedly, thoughtfully, meditatively. He had reached a great climax.

Then, as sometimes happens, a hymn drove home the message with compelling force. The Rev. Philip S. Watters, president of the Hymn Society of America, who was directing the music, made the selection of the hymns which were sung. Realizing how the large company of ministers had been gripped by the words of the address he announced a hymn. In a minute there was a mighty volume of music from those singing preachers whose hearts had been so greatly stirred—

" Ask ye what great thing I know? "

Everyone appeared to sing. Bishop F. J. McConnell, who was presiding, sang with the others. Circumstances made it necessary for Dr. Moldenhawer to return immediately to New York City, and an automobile awaited him at the door of the hotel. He had taken his hat and coat in his hands, and was about to leave the room. But when he heard the first strains of this hymn, he paused, still remained on the platform, and joined heartily in the singing. The writer of this story was one of those present; and he felt, as did the others, that the scene was dramatic and most affecting.

The volume of music appeared to increase as the ministers sang. The questions of their hearts came in every stanza, but the last line always gave the answer—

" Jesus Christ, the Crucified."

The preachers in that great moment were using their imaginations. They realized anew that the Christ who had been crucified could give them victory in life and enable them, and all those to whom they preached, to triumph over death. Their assurance was perfect:

" This is that great thing I know;
This delights and stirs me so:
Faith in Him who died to save,
Him who triumphed o'er the grave,
Jesus Christ, the Crucified."

What Rodeheaver Sang for Anton Lang

Homer Rodeheaver, the far-famed leader of evangelistic song, met Anton Lang about 1930 in Oberammergau. The latter had successfully taken the part of Christ in three presentations of the Passion Play. Lang wanted to hear the American musician sing. So Mr. Rodeheaver sang for the occasion " The Old Rugged Cross."

Mr. Lang listened with delight to the sweet-voiced singer as he began to sing the familiar song of the cross:

> " On a hill far away stood an old rugged cross,
> The emblem of suff'ring and shame."

Particularly was he touched by the last verse:

> " To the old rugged cross I will ever be true,
> Its shame and reproach gladly bear."

" Ah! " said Mr. Lang to Rodeheaver, " that song sums up in the most marvelous way the entire message we are trying to put into the Passion Play which takes us several hours to present."

About that time this song was being acclaimed as one of the most popular pieces of religious music in the United States. Radio stations reported that it mostly led in the requests for favorite religious songs.

Said Matthew Arnold on one occasion, " The cross still makes its ancient appeal to the soul." One realizes that fact when he listens to a great company as it sings

> " So I'll cherish the old rugged cross,
> Till my trophies at last I lay down;
> I will cling to the old rugged cross,
> And exchange it some day for a crown."

Seventeen thousand persons were present at a great gathering in Chicago when this song was sung. People of all classes mingled, and the vast company united in the chorus. Clementine Paddleford, who was present, and later described the scene, reported it in these words: " The roof seemed to rise under the free-sweeping grace of such infinite hope, such a democracy of faith."

The author of this inspiring song, the Rev. George Bennard, was born in Ohio, and spent his early life in Iowa. But when he wrote the song in 1913, he was living in Albion, Michigan.

A radio vote contest was conducted by " Seth Parker " about twenty years after this song was written, and " The Old Rugged Cross " led with twenty-six thousand, six hundred and seventy votes. " Nearer, My God, to Thee," came next with about twenty thousand. Then followed " Abide With Me," " Lead, Kindly Light," and " Rock of Ages."

" With Confidence "

" Arise, my soul, arise;
Shake off thy guilty fears:
The bleeding sacrifice
In my behalf appears:
Before the throne my Surety stands,
My name is written on His hands."

Thus begins one of " Charles Wesley's most jubilant hymns." Often it was sung during the revival meetings conducted by a former generation, and through its agency thousands of persons have surrendered their lives to Christ. Harry Webb Farrington, who himself became a writer of hymns, published an account in *The Christian*

Advocate (December 19, 1929) of the influence of one word in this hymn on his life.

When a lad twelve years of age he lived in Darlington, Maryland, and worked in a mill. But he became interested in some "protracted" meetings held in the Methodist Church. People came from miles around the community, and hitched their horses in the wooden sheds—for the day of the automobile had not arrived.

Following the sermon on Sunday evening, the lad went, with many others, to the "mourner's bench." There knelt the lad, as he prayed for forgiveness. "I knew that I was sorry for my sins and wanted Jesus to forgive me," he said. While on his knees in the crowded church the congregation sang this hymn of Charles Wesley. Nothing happened, however, until the singing company reached the next to the last line in the last verse. The boy listened wonderingly as they sang:

> "With confidence I now draw nigh,
> And, 'Father, Abba, Father,' cry."

When he heard the word "confidence," he seemed to see Jesus. "It was just like being introduced to someone," he said, as he confessed that "from a penitent, weeping boy, I arose happy and smiling. Everybody there knew that something had happened to me. . . . Until that boyhood night I never had the least experience like that before, indeed I had heard about Jesus only two years before."

The emphasis on the word "confidence" had changed a life. The lad himself became a writer of hymns; but his greatest hymn stands related to his experience as a boy of twelve, and its story is the next narrated in this volume.

The Harvard Hymn

Miss Margaret Slattery, whose work is among young people in different parts of the United States, has told the story of the time when she was present at a conference of youth. A young man who was leading the singing read the stanzas of the Harvard Hymn, and remarked, " I think there is real religion in this hymn." As he read it most impressively the young people listened with perfect quiet, which Miss Slattery remarked that she should never forget. It is a short hymn, covering three features: the birth, the crucifixion and the resurrection of Jesus. In each verse the author tells in the opening lines what he does not know; and then, in the third line of the three verses he tells us what he does know. Thus it begins:

> " I know not how that Bethlehem's Babe
> Could in the Godhead be;
> I only know the manger child
> Has brought God's life to me."

Its author, Major Harry Webb Farrington, was born in Nassau, Bahama Islands, July 14, 1880; and died October 25, 1931. His early years were spent working in the mills in Maryland (see the preceding story); but he later secured a broad education. He was a graduate of Syracuse University; of Boston University School of Theology; and was for three years a graduate student in Harvard University. At the outbreak of the World War he went to France, and received an honorary commission.

Greatly interested in work among children, he inaugurated the Week Day Church School at Gary, Indiana, in 1914. He became an ordained minister in the Methodist Church, but he gave a large part of his time, after his return from France, to speaking to the children in the public schools; and in 1929 he said, " I have addressed nearly three million pupils in the public schools of America." He also wrote extensively.

Harvard University in 1910 announced a competition for a Christmas Hymn. The one submitted by Major Farrington received the unanimous vote of the judges, and Professor George Herbert Palmer pronounced it a " perfect poem."

The Harvard Hymn was written in less than thirty minutes, Major Farrington stated. It came out of his experience, and he said that he tried to express himself in the same way as he would have done as a boy of twelve, when he heard the people sing at the " protracted meeting,"

" With confidence I now draw nigh."

Said he, several years after his hymn won the prize, and two years before his death:

" Since then (when the hymn was composed) I have gone through life and have come to my crises and crossroads. It has been at these places that I have felt his (Christ's) intimacy. . . . If I have done anything which bordered on the character of sacrifice . . . it has been because the One who came to me that night at Darlington has made himself one with me at such moments."

His " confidence " in Christ when but twelve years of age led him to sing throughout all the later years, " I know! "

Sung at Jerry McAuley's Funeral

Every foot of available space in the Broadway Tabernacle, New York City, was filled, and hundreds who sought admission were turned away, on Sunday afternoon, September 21, 1884, for the funeral of Jerry McAuley. The people had assembled to honor one who in early life had known the hard way of the transgressor; but who, after his conversion, helped hundreds of others to find the way back from the path of the prodigal to the welcome and forgiveness of the Father. The speakers included Dr. William M. Taylor, pastor of the Broadway Tabernacle Church; Dr. S. Irenaeus Prime, editor of *The New York Observer,* and other prominent clergymen. These distinguished religious leaders paid deserved tribute to Jerry McAuley, the deceased leader of the far-famed Water Street Mission.

The last musical selection rendered by the choir was the one which Jerry most loved. It expressed the experience and the joy of his own life after he had been reclaimed from his wandering ways:

" I will sing of my Redeemer,
    And His wondrous love to me;
On the cruel cross He suffered,
    From the curse to set me free.

" Sing, oh, sing of my Redeemer,
    With His blood He purchased me.
On the cross He sealed my pardon,
    Paid the debt, and made me free."

The song of the mission for the fallen and outcasts, which there reached the souls that had been seared by sin, also found a response when sung in the fashionable church. One who attended that service said: "It was difficult to restrain the pent-up feelings of the heart."

The Irishwoman in Chicago

A woman attending a mission service in Chicago which was conducted by some students from the Moody Bible Institute made a request for the famous hymn of Isaac Watts. So the leader had the audience sing the penetrating words:

> "When I survey the wondrous cross
>   On which the Prince of Glory died,
> My richest gain I count but loss,
>   And pour contempt on all my pride."

The young woman who was in charge was particularly impressed by the person who requested the hymn, and observed that the latter sang every word. "You seem to know that hymn," remarked the evangelist to the visitor at the close of the meeting.

"Yes," answered the woman. "My Sunday-school teacher used to like that hymn. She died, and her last request was that the girls belonging to her class—I was one of them—should get together and sing the hymn." Tears were now streaming down the face of the woman, and she explained that she was an Irishwoman, that she had run away from home, traveled over much of the world as an actress, and was now living an undesirable life. The old hymn, however, brought her mind and heart back to the days before she became wayward. Said the evangelist, "I have reason to believe that she yielded her heart to God."

The evangelist herself had experienced an unusual career. Her story was told in *The Christian Herald,* London, when King George V, on February 23, 1933, conferred on her, at Buckingham Palace, the high honor of membership of the Order of the British Empire.

This woman was Miss Elizabeth Date Davis, M.B.E., of Carlisle, England. Born in Somerset, the daughter of a Cornishman, who was a master mariner, she was led into evangelistic work in 1903, and spent a year at the Moody Bible Institute. Returning to her native England, Miss Davis engaged in mission work in Barnsley, London and elsewhere. At the Methodist Deaconess Institute, she became known as " Sister Lillie," and served as a deaconess at Portsmouth, and later at Cardiff. Said she: " I believe, and have always believed, in the Unseen Presence, and in Divine Guidance—my life, I feel confident, is being guided all the time."

In 1917 she entered on special work in Carlisle. Because of her deep interest in temperance she became, by special arrangement, the organizer of the British Women's Temperance Association in Carlisle. As a later development, in 1923, she started a scheme for taking poor children for a day's outing to the seaside, and her friends provided a camp which became known as the " Sister Lillie Shelter " at Silloth.

Many experiences of great interest have come to this remarkable woman, but one of the most treasured incidents is that of the woman in Chicago who sang

" When I survey the wondrous cross,"

and then told her life-story with tear-filled eyes.

Wanted More of That Singing

" And can it be that I should gain
An interest in the Saviour's blood?
Died He for me, who caused His pain?
For me, who Him to death pursued?
Amazing love! how can it be
That Thou, my Lord, shouldst die for me? "

A moment of great exultation came to the English
Methodist Conference which met in Bristol in the summer of 1935. This city is closely identified with early
Methodism, and particularly with Charles Wesley and his
hymns. Anglican and Free Church representatives welcomed this gathering to the city at one of the sessions,
and among those who spoke was the Dean of Bristol. The
speeches were ended, and the Conference rose to sing
Charles Wesley's hymn to the tune of *Sagina,* " And can
it be? "

The Dean remained to pronounce the benediction.
Meantime something of a very arresting nature happened.
Several writers reported the scene. Said one: " How we
sang it! The men's voices on the floor of the hall, and the
women's up in the galleries, rolled out the great old hymn
in one glorious harmony. I watched the Dean. . . . Oh,
how he listened. When it was over he pronounced the
benediction. Then he smiled and said, ' I wish you'd come
and sing like that in our churches.' "

Another correspondent, writing of the " Conference in
Song," said, as he referred to this hymn: " Now watch
the Dean. In verse one (there are five verses in the English Hymn Book), with bowed head, he seemed to be
weighing his judgment of Charles Wesley's theology. In
verse two his chin no longer rested on a silk-clad chest. In

verse three the melody caught him in its sweep, and he sang verse four with radiant face."

A third writer declared, as he also spoke of the impression made on the Dean by this hymn, "The lyrical passion bursts into song there as scarcely anywhere else."

"These verses no doubt describe Charles Wesley's own conversion," says the Rev. John Telford. On the last Sunday of the earthly life of John Wesley he engaged in a brief conversation with Miss Ritchie. He was very weak. She quoted to him the words which close this hymn:

> "Bold I approach the eternal throne,
> And claim the crown, through Christ my own."

The dying man responded: "He is all, He is all." Then he added: "I will go."

CHAPTER XII

"CROWN HIM" IN SONG

" One generation after another is bound together by a golden chain of praise."—" *The Evolution of the English Hymn*," by *F. J. Gillman.*

" Over four thousand people attended a meeting at the Municipal Auditorium in St. Paul, Minnesota, to sing the great hymns of the Christian Church. There were no tickets, no charge or collection. A narrator traced the development of the great hymns, and how they came to be born. Men sang the clarion calls, and women the hymns of faith. All the churches in the city united for this first service of the ' Singing Church.' Ten church choirs sang, and a large Negro chorus filled the hall with old spirituals."—" *Reader's Digest*," *July, 1935.*

" As the great congregation closed the morning service I could not see a soul who was not singing. The deep full-toned organ was almost drowned in its majestic accompaniment, as those matchless words of the great English hymn closed:

" ' Were the whole realm of nature mine,
That were an offering far too small;
Love so amazing, so divine,
Demands my soul, my life, my all.'

" After the benediction and quiet spell of silent prayer, the organ chimed out the refrain and the congregation moved reverently out. An aged woman came with others toward the foot of the pulpit. As she spoke quietly to her pastor, her trembling hand took his; her eyes were dimmed with tears, and she said, ' I feel I have been with Him this morning. That last hymn opened the portals for me.'

" What a benediction ! "—*Dr. John Timothy Stone.*

158

Crowned Christ Where Druids Once Assembled

" Unique " was the word used by a man who made a journey of 125 miles on his motor-cycle to attend a service of worship at Carn Brea, Cornwall, as he described in *The British Weekly* the gathering held on an August day in 1930. The location was sketched as " the last hill in England—probably used from prehistoric days, through Druidical times, down to the present for worship." Miners from the surrounding towns and hamlets, and fishermen from the coast communities, gathered from far and near that they might attend this open-air service. The location is just a short distance from the famous Gwennap Pit where John Wesley preached to vast congregations, and where on each Whit-Monday a service is still held.

Cornishmen love to sing. Therefore it was a great moment when the assembled company lifted up their voices in song. The singing was led by the Salvation Army Band of Penzance, who had made a trip of several miles for the occasion. Oddly enough, one of the members of the band that day wore the uniform of Newark, New Jersey. Probably he was a Cornishman who had settled in the United States, and was back in his native county for a summer vacation.

It is always a thrilling sensation to hear a Cornish congregation in its own place of worship sing, to the tune of Miles Lane,

> " All hail the power of Jesus' Name!
> Let angels prostrate fall;
> Bring forth the royal diadem,
> And crown Him Lord of all."

There on that historic hill came moments of ecstasy as

the voices blended with the band in singing the last stanza of the " most inspiring and triumphant hymn in the English language ":

> " O that with yonder sacred throng
>   We at His feet may fall!
> We'll join the everlasting song,
>   And crown Him Lord of all."

Four Thousand Persons Sang Communion Hymn

Hundreds of men and women were waiting for admission at Keswick, England, in the summer of 1934, on the night when the sacrament of the Lord's Supper was to be administered. Four thousand people seated themselves in the twenty minutes which were allowed between the opening of the doors and the beginning of the service. " Surely this was the largest gathering for such a purpose in any one place," remarked one who was present. Not a seat was vacant, and people continued standing round the fringes of the huge tent. There were moments of profound silence during the service which were characterized as being " almost oppressive."

The service, however, closed with a joyous outburst of song, as the vast company, who had remembered the broken body and shed blood of their Lord, triumphantly sang:

> " Crown Him with many crowns,
>   The Lamb upon His throne;
> Hark! how the heavenly anthem drowns
>   All music but its own.
> Awake, my soul, and sing
>   Of Him who died for Thee
> And hail Him as thy matchless King
>   Through all eternity."

Matthew Bridges, the author of this hymn, was born in Malden, Essex, England, July 14, 1800; and died in Quebec, Canada, October 6, 1894. His early life was spent in the Church of England, but in mid-life he became a Roman Catholic.

A historic incident has been preserved for us by the Rev. John Telford, who wrote: "At the Bible Society's Centenary Thanksgiving in the Royal Albert Hall, London (November, 1905), after congratulatory messages had been read from all the Protestant rulers of Christendom, the Marquis of Northampton, who presided over the meeting, said: 'Now that we have read these addresses from earthly rulers, let us turn our mind to the King of kings. We will sing, "Crown Him with Many Crowns."'"

Scots Sang with Uplifted Hands

" I'm not ashamed to own my Lord,
Or to defend His cause,
Maintain the glory of His Cross
And honor all His laws."

Extraordinary scenes were witnessed in Coatbridge, Scotland, in the early part of 1938 during the campaign of the Churches' Recall to Religion. In a news note to *The British Weekly* an unsigned writer thus reported: " The great Town Hall has been taxed to its utmost capacity, and hundreds have been unable to get in. Churches have been crowded out. Young people's meetings have been full to overflowing. Meetings for men have resulted in marvelous attendances. Never within memory has there been such a response, and every possible type of person has been touched." The Rev. F. W. Norwood, D.D., a former pastor of the great City Temple, London, was the special evangelistic preacher during the campaign.

The mission was concluded on a Sunday night in the Town Hall. This building was crowded, and an overflow meeting was held in a large church. " Altogether . . . more than four thousand people must have been listening to the preacher." Dr. Norwood stressed the need both for Christian living and service. Toward the close, " with right hands uplifted the huge concourse sang the first verse of the fifty-fourth Paraphrase, ' I'm not ashamed to own my Lord.' "

An incident comes to us through the Rev. John Telford concerning this hymn of Isaac Watts. It tells of an aged minister whose mind was failing, who was visited by a friend. " Well," said the latter, " I see you do not know *me;* do you know *Jesus,* whom I serve in the gospel? "

Hearing the word Jesus, the sick man started and looked up, as if just aroused from sleep; then, lifting his eyes, he exclaimed, as he began to repeat the second verse of this hymn:

> " Jesus my Lord! I know His Name;
> His Name is all my boast."

Star and Song

Ten thousand people, it was estimated, were crowded into the great auditorium at Ocean Grove, New Jersey, on an occasion when a Summer School of Religious Education presented a pageant, in July, 1922.

A moment came when a great electric star flashed forth, framing the word JESUS in the center, and bearing in its five points the words, " Wonderful," " Counsellor," "Mighty God," "Everlasting Father," "Prince of Peace."

At that instant the great audience rose and joined the chorus choir, with a feeling of happy exultation, in singing:

> "Let every kindred, every tribe,
> On this terrestrial ball,
> To Him all majesty ascribe,
> And crown Him Lord of all."

The great outburst of song, rendered by those who rejoiced in Jesus as "The Light of the World," created a profound impression on all present, and many continued to speak of it long afterward. It was an inspirational (one might almost safely say an inspired) rendering of one of the gripping stanzas of Perronet's triumphant hymn—

> "All hail the power of Jesus' Name."

CHAPTER XIII

SONGS OF HEAVENWARD SOARING SOULS

"Why do we sing hymns on heaven and the future life?" said a youth to me with the blood pulsing like fire through the veins. I answered, "They are not for you. But wait a bit. One day someone very dear to you will pass within the veil; some day you will dip down to the brink of the cold river, yourself; and then you will be ready enough for hymns on heaven, and be thankful that they are retained in the hymn book."
—The Rev. A. E. Witham.

"It is the privilege of every child of God to live in heaven before he gets there."*—The Rev. F. Luke Wiseman, D.D.*

A minister attended the funeral of an older clergyman. The former did not think the hymns sung were sufficiently assuring. Said he: "I was born into a stronger tradition of faith. I went home and wrote a note that those who bury me will find one day with my will. I ask that they shall sing for me:

"'One family we dwell in Him,
One church above, beneath,
Though now divided by the stream,
The narrow stream of death.

"'One army of the living God,
To His command we bow:
Part of His host have crossed the flood,
And part are crossing now.'"
—The Recorder.

"Heaven is pictured as a place of song. Why not make earth heaven by using it aright?

164

" ' Ten thousand times ten thousand
　In sparkling raiment bright,
The armies of the ransomed saints
　Throng up the steeps of light.' "
　　　　　　　　—*Dr. John Timothy Stone.*

Sankey Remembered by What He Sang

" Fading away like the stars of the morning,
    Losing their light in the glorious sun—
Thus would we pass from the earth and its toiling,
    Only remembered by what we have done.

" Only remembered, only remembered,
    Only remembered by what we have done;
    Thus would we pass from the earth and its toiling,
    Only remembered by what we have done."

The words of this hymn were written by Dr. Horatius Bonar, the prolific hymn writer of Scotland, and it was set to music by Ira D. Sankey in 1891. Said Mr. Sankey: " I sang it as a solo in the Tabernacle in London at the funeral of my friend, C. H. Spurgeon, the great London preacher." The lines are based on Psalm 45: 17: " I will make thy name to be remembered."

A visit was made by Dr. Charles E. Locke (who afterward became a bishop), when he was pastor in Brooklyn, to Mr. Sankey. It was a memorable afternoon. The sweet singer of Israel was reposing on a couch in a room flooded with the golden sunlight of the waning day. Cataracts had brought blindness to Mr. Sankey, and his form had wasted away. But, as usual, he was in a cheerful mood.

The visitor informed Mr. Sankey that at the evening service on the previous Sunday, at the Hansom Street Church, the congregation had sung nothing but the songs associated with his name. There were " The Ninety and Nine," " There'll Be No Dark Valley," and others.

Deeply gratified by the message which had been brought to him, the face of the blind singer became illuminated, and he said, " I can sing a little yet." Then he continued, " I will sing you the song which I sang at the funeral of Spurgeon in London." Said Bishop Locke, as he related the incident to a large audience at Atlantic City, New Jersey, in May, 1932, " With infinite pathos he sang all the verses of ' Only Remembered by What I Have Done.' "

Both men were touched by emotion as they bade each other good-bye. The visitor told Mr. Sankey that he would be back again soon. What followed was thus related by Bishop Locke:

" A few days later, unexpectedly, he did ' steal away gently and lovingly.' Mrs. Sankey asked me to take charge of the funeral services. There was a great company of bereaved friends, and there were many appropriate addresses. In my remarks I recalled the little episode which I have here described, and then said: ' Yes, Mr. Sankey has gone; only remembered by what he has *sung.*' "

Closed Life with a Chorus

One who had been active in the service of Christ, and who used his manly voice to make music unto the Lord, was laid low with a serious illness while yet in the prime of life. A member of the family told me how the man had been unable to speak above a low whisper for several hours. But, eventually, he made known to members of the watching group that he wanted some of them to sing —for the family was a musical one.

One selection after another was attempted, but each time the sick man shook his head. It was not the song he wished. But he could not make the singers understand just what he desired. Finally a bit of inspiration came to one, for he knew that his father loved the gospel song:

> " When peace like a river attendeth my way,
>   When sorrows like sea billows roll,
>   Whatever my lot, Thou hast taught me to say:
>   It is well, it is well with my soul."

When the son began to sing these lines, the dying father nodded his approval. But when the chorus was reached all those in the room were amazed as the man on his sick bed, with a clear voice, joined with others in singing:

> " It is well with my soul,
>   It is well, it is well with my soul! "

The music ceased. Quietly the man composed himself. In a short time he was not, for God had taken him to Himself.

Had Reached the Last Verse

Some hymns go with us through life, and occasionally one expresses the changing experiences which come with the passing of the years. One of the very beautiful stories of hymns relating themselves to human life was reported by the Rev. Noel F. Hutchcroft, a skilled leader of song, in *The Methodist Recorder.* " A Bit of Life," this English minister called the incident which he heard related by the chairman of a West of England Song Festival. The latter stated that he was at one time the leader of a Brotherhood meeting of pronounced evangelistic spirit; and the members of the organization assigned themselves the task of winning for Christ one of the worst men of the community.

Eventually he was won, and in the first days of his changed life he asked for a copy of the song book used in the meetings conducted by the Brotherhood.

Years of consistent living followed, during which faithful service for Christ was rendered. Then came illness. " The leader visited him and found him reading—a chorus hymn! "

> " I will sing the wondrous story
>   Of the Christ who died for me;
> How He left His home in glory,
>   For the cross on Calvary.

> " Yes, I'll sing the wondrous story
>   Of the Christ who died for me—
> Sing it with the saints in glory,
>   Gathered by the crystal sea."

The sick man pointed to some lines of the hymn, and said, " Ye know, sir, that's me! " Then he read:

> " I was lost; but Jesus found me—
>   Found the sheep that went astray."

The man grew worse as the days lengthened into weeks and months. Finally, when the home-call was near, the leader found him still reading his beloved song, though he was almost too weak to bear the weight of the book.

" Still the same hymn, Jack? " asked the visitor.

" Aye; same hymn," was the reply; " but I've reached the last verse now." Then he quoted the closing stanza:

> " He will keep me till the river
>   Rolls its waters at my feet;
> Then He'll bear me safely over,
>   Where the loved ones I shall meet."

Religion Made a Dying Man Sing

Following the establishment of a mission at Singapore by the Methodist Episcopal Church, in 1884, a school was opened which immediately drew a large student body. C. A. Gray went from Zanesville, Ohio, to take charge of this school, and in ten weeks was taken seriously ill. The physician told this young man, to the surprise of both himself and his friends, that he soon would die. Thinking it over, he faced the situation calmly. Then he said to the Rev. W. F. Oldham (later Bishop Oldham), "Call in the boys." Forty boys from Malaysia and Siam soon entered the presence of the sick man in a body.

According to the story, as related by Dr. Albert Osborn in his biography of Bishop J. F. Hurst, the teacher said: "Boys, I have sent for you to let you see how a Christian can die. I want you to pass by and let me grasp each of you by the hand." Then, while the boys were greeting their teacher, the sick man began to sing, all alone (for the others were so overcome that they could not sing):

"Down at the cross where my Saviour died,
Down where for cleansing from sin I cried,
There to my heart was the blood applied;
Glory to His name."

When vacation time came, Dr. Oldham went into Java to interview some new students. While there he took dinner at the home of an old man. Sitting at the table was the oldest son of the host; and also a youth who related the incident of the man who sang when he was dying. Greatly agitated, the boy's grandfather took Dr. Oldham by the coat, and said to him in the presence of the assembled company: " Do you see that boy? That is my grandson. He is the light of these old eyes. Take him and fill him full of that religion that makes a man sing when he dies."

Smiles Shining Through Tears

A happy preacher was Bishop William A. Quayle, and he radiated happiness wherever he went. Like his Master, he greatly loved people—" folks," he called them. A master of pulpit eloquence in an unusual form, a keen student both of books and nature, he still found time to do much visiting among his congregations when he was a pastor. His experiences while associating with others afforded him an endless variety of illustrations for his sermons.

The story of the visit he made to a brother preacher who was dying was sometimes related by him, and has also been recorded in one of the many books he wrote. He tried, " with tremulous voice," he said, to sing for the sick man—

> " If, on a quiet sea,
> Toward heaven we calmly sail
> With grateful hearts, O God, to Thee,
> We'll own the favoring gale."

Closed were the eyes of the dying minister as he listened. Tears ran down his cheeks and dropped on his pillow, " for his weak hand could not wipe the tears away, through they were happy tears." The veteran of the cross was soaring heavenward on the wings of sacred song.

The voice of the singing preacher continued—

> " But should the surges rise,
> And rest delay to come,
> Blest be the tempest, kind the storm,
> Which drives us nearer home."

Bishop Quayle affirmed that he never heard a sweeter " Amen " than that which came from the smiling lips of the man who was nearing the painless life of the Celestial City. " His eyes were wide open now. While tears were in them, smiles were shining through the tears like sunlight through the rain."

Four Joyful Old Men

Those four old men, all of whom I knew, joined in the birthday dinner for one of their number, and then spent a happy afternoon together. The average age of this congenial company was over fourscore. Three were ministers, and were now retired; and one was a devoted layman. Two were veterans of the Civil War. All belonged to the same denomination. Each had a good appetite, and a store of choice memories. Life had brought them heavy responsibilities, but they had " kept the faith." Now they had reached " the long last mile."

Before they parted, they joined in repeating the twenty-third Psalm; and then they sang the Doxology. Christians and patriots, veterans of the cross and of their country, with Thanksgiving only a week ahead, they could unite with each other, as they had often done with their several congregations, in singing:

> " Praise God, from whom all blessings flow;
> Praise Him, all creatures here below;
> Praise Him above, ye heavenly host;
> Praise Father, Son, and Holy Ghost."

Their voices may have been slightly cracked, and they may have faltered just a little; but they had not forgotten the fine art of praise. The spirit of gratitude for God's leadership during a long life, which was often expressed in conversation during the afternoon, now voiced itself in song. Then they all bowed in prayer. First the one whose birthday was being observed offered prayer; then each of the others followed.

Would they meet again? Perhaps not, on earth. But surely they would all meet again. Their hope was radiant, and their Easter faith triumphant. What was more natural than that they should voice their faith once more in song? They did. The little parlor rang with the voices of those heroes as they sang the song of other days which was so comfortingly suggestive:

> " There's a land that is fairer than day,
>   And by faith we can see it afar;
> For the Father waits over the way,
>   To prepare us a dwelling-place there.
>
>   .   .   .   .   .
>
> " To our bountiful Father above,
>   We will offer our tribute of praise
> For the glorious gift of His love,
>   And the blessings that hallow our days.
>
>   " In the sweet by and by,
>   We shall meet on that beautiful shore;
>   In the sweet by and by,
>   We shall meet on that beautiful shore."

A transfiguring glow was upon the faces of those fou' aged men, and just a bit of moisture in their somewh' dim eyes, when they began to shake hands before th' separated. " The best is yet to be," said one as he tended his hand. Probably the words of Browning were in his mind:

> " Grow old along with me!
> The best is yet to be,
> The last of life, for which the first was made."

As I write these words in 1939, I think of all four, the funerals of some of whom I attended—for all have gone to their coronation. One was over ninety-nine years of age when for him came the last " clear call." They have met " on that beautiful shore," of which they so hopefully and courageously sang.

Those four men are no longer old. They are eternally young.

" Sing Them to God "

In the last article that she wrote for *The Silver Cross,* Mrs. Margaret Bottome, founder of The International Order of the King's Daughters and Sons, related some of her experiences while visiting the South. One secretary told her of a Circle of colored children, whose name was, " We Sing Them to God." That seemed to be a strange name, but the reason given was the following: " When anyone dies, or the doctor says they cannot live, then the Circle is sent for to sing them to God." Only the night before they had been singing

> " Nearer, my God, to Thee "

for one who was sick. Commenting on this fact, Mrs. Bottome added her own remarkable experience in these words:

" We need not wait for people to die to sing them to God, though I think it is lovely to sing to them then. I remember going to sing day after day to a beautiful woman—a stranger to me—who sent for me to come and sing to her as day after day she went, step by step, down into the Valley—and when I would say, ' What shall I sing for you today? ' she would smile and answer, ' Rock of Ages.' And one day it was sung for the last time. Of course I attended the funeral, and thought I would like to look at her face once more. I shall never forget how startled I was to see her on her side and there was the hymn book and her finger pointing to ' Rock of Ages.' How glad I was that for so many days I had sung her to God."

So impressed was Dr. James M. Buckley by this incident that he quoted it in an extended tribute to Mrs. Bottome, with whom he had a close acquaintance, in *The Christian Advocate.*

CHAPTER XIV

SINGING IN THE HOME

" Music is a tonic for the tired and weary mind,
   It's comfort for the lonely, and it's pictures to the blind!
   It's sympathy and laughter, and it's faith and mirth, and
      prayer,
   It's kindness in its brightest dress, and it's welcomed
      everywhere."

—*Edgar A. Guest.*

Speaking of his mother, Henry Turner Bailey said in " Yankee
Notions ": " How vividly I see her even now, after more than
fifty years, with the firelight on her lovely face, and Baby Charlie
in her arms, as we sat around the hearth of a Sunday evening
in the gloaming singing together the songs of Zion:

" ' Guide me, O Thou great Jehovah,
   Pilgrim through this barren land;
   I am weak, but Thou art mighty;
   Hold me with Thy powerful hand.' "

" In visions does it not come over you—the evenings when
around the little cabinet organ with your mother you used to
sing, ' Is my name written there? ' ' Safe in the arms of Jesus.'
. . . Only the music of heaven can make melody in the soul."

—*The Rev. Elmer E. Helms, D.D.*

" There is much for which I give thanks as I remember the
home of my childhood in New England. But one of the most
vivid and loved memories is of the Sunday evenings when we
would sit and sing as the daylight died away. We sang some
strange hymns. . . . Yet the memory even of those is sweet.
I never read or think of David's combat with Goliath, without

176

recalling how my father loved the stirring song which began,
' Strike the cymbal,' and then went on to describe how

> " ' From the river,
> Rejected quiver,
> Judah's hero takes the stone;
> Spread your banners,
> Shout hosannas;
> The battle is the Lord's alone.'

"Probably nowhere but in New England would ' banners '
be set to rhyme with ' hosannas '; but there it did not seem in-
congruous. And I can recall the thrill that came as we sang of
that conflict in which right won against might through the power
of the unseen God."—*The Rev. William P. Merrill, D.D., on
"The Religious Value of Hymns." (The Papers of the Hymn
Society of America.)*

Mother's Face When She Sang

Touchingly beautiful was the tribute which Dr. Daniel A. Poling paid to his mother in *The Christian Herald,* in October, 1937, after she had gone to her coronation. Heading it, "Mother—1857–1937," he wrote these words:

"I found her in that far-away where a child's memory begins —and she was singing.

"Fragments of those songs come to me now. One she sang to a dying President, James Garfield.

"'My Father is rich in houses and lands,
He holdeth the wealth of the world in His hands!
Of rubies and diamonds, of silver and gold,
His coffers are full—He has riches untold.'

"Always when mother sang that song her face became luminous with the light that never was on land or sea. We heard her sing it for the last time only a little while ago as she sat in her chair and we gathered about her. Now evermore she sings it with the chorus of her 'Beulah-land.'"

Many of us have seen the faces of others of God's saintly children grow luminous as they have sung this song with the note of confidence found in the chorus:

"I'm the child of a King, the child of a King!
With Jesus, my Saviour, I'm the child of a King."

Earliest Memory of Mother's Singing

Snow lay deep on the ground, and the wintry winds of Northern New York were blowing bleakly on a February afternoon when I listened to "Joe Emerson and His

Choir" in their radio program of "Hymns of All Churches." Mr. Emerson announced that the first hymn to be sung that afternoon was the first hymn he remembered his mother singing. His listeners, too, he intimated, probably had memories of their own mothers singing this or other beloved hymns. So, for mother's sake, those listening were invited to join the little choir as they sang in their studio:

> " O happy day, that fixed my choice
> On Thee, my Saviour and my God!
> Well may this glowing heart rejoice,
> And tell its raptures all abroad."

Sitting quietly in their own homes doubtless many accepted the invitation of the leader, and joined in singing the refrain with the unseen singers:

> " Happy day, happy day,
> When Jesus washed my sins away:
> He taught me how to watch and pray,
> And live rejoicing every day.
> Happy day, happy day,
> When Jesus washed my sins away."

Doubtless while listening, or perhaps also singing this song which was dear to the heart of the mother of the leader, some thought of their own mothers of thirty or fifty years ago. Mothers of that distant period who had neither radio nor telephone, would go about their household tasks of sweeping, dusting and baking, singing the songs of an earlier day which they learned in church service, Sunday school and revival meeting. And, among them all, none was more familiar, easier to sing, or brought greater happiness than " Happy Day."

Song Services in the White House

President William McKinley, a devout Christian, was fond of hearing sung the stately old hymns of the church, and enjoyed singing with others. Sunday evenings, during his residence in Washington, he was accustomed to have a group of intimate friends gather at the White House for a service of sacred song. Sunday mornings Mr. McKinley attended church services alone, as the state of Mrs. McKinley's health did not permit her to accompany him. But in the evening he would remain with her.

Not only did President and Mrs. McKinley mingle their voices with those of their guests, but Mrs. McKinley would occasionally play the accompaniment. These informal home services began before Mr. McKinley became President, in fact. A frequent guest at these gatherings was Bishop John F. Hurst, who resided in Washington at that time, and who was the first chancellor of the American University.

President McKinley had his personal hymn book, which he used on these occasions. " Lead, Kindly Light " was often sung, because of the President's love for the same. But the hymn in which he most delighted was:

> " Nearer, my God, to Thee,
> Nearer to Thee! "

This hymn gave expression to the prayer of his heart and the desire of his life.

Burdened with many cares, he still could drop them all on Sunday evenings and join with his assembled friends in singing:

" Still all my song shall be,
Nearer, my God, to Thee,
Nearer to Thee! "

When came the untimely end, and the shadows were gathering round him, though he could no longer sing his beloved hymn, yet he whispered the words, " Nearer to Thee! "

CHAPTER XV

CHILDHOOD SONGS

When *The British Weekly*, in 1933, asked for the favorite hymns for children, the replies indicated that the song which led all others was

" Jesus loves me, this I know,
For the Bible tells me so."

The prayer for childhood which was given first place consisted of these lines:

"Gentle Jesus, meek and mild,
Look upon a little child.
Pity my simplicity,
Suffer me to come to Thee."

Sir William Robertson Nicoll went with his father, who was a Scottish minister, to some revival meetings, when he was quite small. But he always declared afterward that the hymns sung at those revival services made a deep impression on his mind. " Teach a little child hymns," he would often say, " as the beginning of its theology."

" ' Rabbi ' Duncan, at one time professor of Hebrew in New College, Edinburgh, and a man of vast learning in Oriental tongues, was suspected by his students of offering his private prayers in Hebrew. It is said that two of them determined to prove the truth or falsehood of this rumor, by listening outside his bedroom door after he retired for the night. Everything went according to plan. They heard the old scholar potter about his room for some minutes, and then kneel down to pray. But it was no Hebrew that came. The erudite old saint just said:

" ' Gentle Jesus, meek and mild,
Look upon a little child.
Pity my simplicity,
Suffer me to come to Thee.'

That was all. His deep prayer had been offered earlier in the day, and with a fresh mind. He committed himself to God at the last with the simple words of childhood. The listeners heard the bed creak and knew that 'Rabbi' Duncan had gone to sleep."—*The Rev. W. E. Sangster in "The Methodist Recorder."*

When Children Sang at Northfield

Impressive was the experience which came to Dr. Floyd W. Tomkins, a scholarly and saintly clergyman of Philadelphia, when he preached during the summer of 1922 in East Northfield. Just before he began his sermon in the great auditorium which D. L. Moody erected for the purpose of housing the summer conferences for Christian workers, a group of children sang one of the songs they had learned. These youngsters, from the crowded sections of New York City, had been brought up to Northfield in order that they might spend a week in the country.

Sitting together in a section of the building, they were presented to the congregation for the purpose of singing a song. One little girl sang the verses of the hymn by Emily E. S. Elliott:

> " Thou didst leave Thy throne and Thy kingly crown,
>> When Thou camest to earth for me;
>> But in Bethlehem's home there was found no room
>> For Thy holy Nativity.
>> O come to my heart, Lord Jesus,
>> There is room in my heart for Thee."

But whenever she reached the closing lines of the verses, all the children joined with the soloist in singing:

> " O come to my heart, Lord Jesus,
>> There is room in my heart for Thee."

Describing this occasion afterward in *The Sunday School Times,* Dr. Tomkins said: " It was difficult for me to preach for a moment; the message had already been given out of the mouth of God's little ones."

Heard Little Girl Singing to Her Dolly

The sweet voice of a little girl was heard as she sang to her dolly, though she knew not that anyone was listening. But a woman sat by her window in a town in Colorado that day who later confessed that she was "too discouraged to read, too tired to do fancywork, too weary even to think." She it was who heard the song of the little girl who was "playing house." Later (December 21, 1911) the woman recorded her experience in *The Christian Endeavor World*.

This woman had moved from her home in the East because of signs of tuberculosis. Even in her Western home, however, she did not appear to be regaining her health. Then, at a critical period, came to her ears the song of the child:

> " Jesus bids us shine
>   With a pure, clear light,
> Like a little candle
>   Burning in the night.
> In this world of darkness,
>   So let us shine,
> You in your small corner,
>   And I in mine."

The sick woman, not long married, found the words repeating themselves—"And I in mine." Then she began to ask herself, "What am I doing? How am I shining?" She began to think of the past few months, and realized that she had become self-centered, and confessed that she had reached the point where she was "selfish and discontented."

After relating the incident to her husband, and talking over matters, they moved out into the open country.

There they found good neighbors, and attended the simple services in the country schoolhouse. The woman became more interested in life generally. Slowly she began to gain in weight, and the power to sleep. Her husband worked the land, and the sick woman found herself able to assist in the home. Said she, in relating the story of her later life, " The simple life on the plains . . . has taught us to value more highly the things worth while in life. . . . It has brought the longed-for health, and has made life one grand, sweet song for me." Then she indicated that she had come to a realization of the fact that " it is the little things that really count in life."

The woman's changed attitude toward life came at the moment when a child singing her Sunday-school song to her dolly unconsciously conveyed a note of hope and courage to a despondent spirit.

This song appears in the section devoted to hymns " For Little Children " in " The Hymnary " of the United Church of Canada, and is likewise found in " The New Canadian Hymnal."

True it is:

> " Jesus bids us shine,
>   First of all for Him;
> Well He sees and knows it,
>   If our light grows dim:
> He looks down from heaven
>   To see us shine,
> You in your small corner,
>   And I in mine."

Children's Hospital Became a Temple

One Sunday evening the head nurse of an English hospital was reading Bible stories to the children, and showing them pictures. Soon they began to sing, and some of the children asked for the " Little Friend Hymn." The nurse played it over; and one of the girls who had recently arrived, a little invalid, said: " Oh, Nurse, may I sing that, please! We learned it in our Sunday school."

The nurse gave her consent. Some of the children were sitting up in their beds, the soloist among the number. Those who were too weak to sit up were asked to lift their hands whenever the singer reached the line, in both the first and the last verses, " I am Jesu's little friend." Gleefully, despite their disability, the children entered into the spirit of the hymn. The evening was very quiet, and the sweet, piping voice of the singer sounded out clearly:

> " I am Jesu's little friend,
> On His mercy I depend:
> If I try to please Him ever,
> If I grieve His Spirit never,
> O how very good to me
> Will my Saviour always be!
>
> .   .   .   .   .   .
>
> " He is with me all the day,
> With me in my busy play;
> O'er my waking and my sleeping
> Jesus still a watch is keeping;
> I can lay me down and rest,
> Sweetly pillowed on His breast."

" As I looked down the whole length of the ward, and saw all the thin white hands held up, and thought what they meant, it was almost too much for me," said the nurse who reported the incident in *The Christian Herald*, London. " The ward became a holy temple, as I thought

I could see our Lord going from child to child, taking each by the hand, saying, ' My little friend.' "

This cheerful song for children is found in " The New Canadian Hymnal," published by the United Church Publishing House of Toronto, and the selection is credited to Frances J. Crosby. The words are associated with " Danish Melody," arranged by C. L. Naylor. It is a lovely song for childhood, and one does not wonder that hospital children found joy as they sang

" I am Jesu's little friend."

Alyce's Prayer Hymn Before the Operation

Among the two thousand letters which reached ten-year-old Alyce Jane McHenry in March, 1935, just before and immediately following her serious operation, was one sent to her by Johnny Steinburger. Johnny, also ten years of age, wrote from a hospital in Brooklyn. During his short life he had gone through nineteen operations, and had spent four years in various hospitals in Kansas City, Albany and New York. Alyce, who was from Omaha, Nebraska, underwent a critical operation for an unusual disorder at Fall River, Massachusetts. Her case was front-page news for the papers for a few days, and from those various accounts the story of the hymn was gleaned.

Alyce told the nurses about Johnny's letter when she was reported to be making satisfactory progress toward recovery. She said that Johnny Steinburger, in his letter, told her not to forget to say her prayers before the operation. In fact, he copied one for her, as follows:

" Jesus, tender Shepherd, hear me,
Bless Thy little lamb tonight;
Through the darkness be Thou near me;
Keep me safe till morning light."

Where Johnny learned this hymn which he recommended to his fellow sufferer, it would be interesting to know. But evidently the little fellow had learned the value of this prayer hymn for childhood.

The hymn was written by Mary Lundie Duncan early in the last century. Its author, a native of Scotland, was the daughter of one minister and the wife of another. Her younger sister married the renowned Scottish minister, Dr. Horatius Bonar, who made choice contributions to the hymnody of the Christian Church.

This beautiful hymn for childhood is found in " The Hymnal " of the Protestant Episcopal Church, and also in " The Hymnal " of the Presbyterian Church. It " holds a unique place among evening hymns for children. In every word it breathes the childlike spirit."

The other stanzas indicate how appropriate it is for an evening song or prayer for childhood, especially the second which teaches the child to say:

" All this day Thy hand has led me,
And I thank Thee for Thy care;
Thou hast clothed me, warmed and fed me;
Listen to my evening prayer."

CHAPTER XVI

HYMNS OF YOUTH

" In a little church I learned to sing,

> " ' How firm a foundation, ye saints of the Lord,
> Is laid for your faith in His excellent word! '

This hymn has done for me more than could have done a score
of college diplomas."—*The Hon. James J. Davis.*

> " Almighty Lord, with one accord
> We offer Thee our youth,
> And pray that Thou would'st give us now
> The warfare of the truth.

> . . . . . .

> " Let fall on every college hall
> The luster of Thy cross,
> That love may dare Thy work to share
> And count all else as loss.

> " Our hearts be ruled, our spirits schooled
> Alone Thy will to seek;
> And when we find Thy blessed mind,
> Instruct our lips to speak."
> —*M. Woolsey Stryker.*

This hymn, says Dr. Elmer A. Leslie in *Zion's Herald,* is pre-
eminently adapted to use in a college, yet it is fitting for student life anywhere. It represents the students singing, offering
their lives, enlisting in the warfare for the truth.

" Then comes a twofold prayer. First, may not the shadow but
the lustre of Christ's cross fall upon every college hall. Second,
teach us how to find the mind of Christ, and having found it
to speak out in accordance with it."

190

Youth's Own Hymn

Eight lines of religious poetry have placed Howard Arnold Walter among the immortals, though he died in India at the age of thirty-five. His lines, set to music, have proved to be one of the most appealing hymns for young people.

The author was born in New Britain, Connecticut, in 1883, and was a brilliant student at Princeton University, where he graduated with honors, and at Hartford Seminary. Soon he went to Japan, and on July 1, 1906, he wrote a poem and sent it to his mother. It was his personal message to her. But she wisely shared it with others by sending it to *Harper's Magazine,* where it appeared in 1907. What could be more expressive of a sturdy resolution to live nobly and usefully than these eight lines?

> " I would be true, for there are those who trust me;
> I would be pure, for there are those who care;
> I would be strong, for there is much to suffer;
> I would be brave, for there is much to dare.
>
> " I would be friend of all—the foe, the friendless;
> I would be giving and forget the gift;
> I would be humble, for I know my weakness;
> I would look up, and laugh, and love, and lift."

Returning to the United States, the young man continued his education in Hartford Seminary, and was ordained into the ministry of the Congregational Church. In 1912 he went to India to serve the Young Men's Christian Association; and there, in 1918, he died during the influenza epidemic. This young adventurer for Christ met the greatest adventure by saying, " O Christ, I am ready." A tablet has been placed in his home church in Great Britain on which the entire hymn is inscribed.

Bishop John H. Vincent had the wise habit of copying short bits of poetry and prose in little notebooks which he carried in his vest pockets. These he would quote on appropriate occasions to great advantage. He evidently saw the poem of Mr. Walter soon after its publication, and was impressed by the same. More than once did I hear the venerable and beloved founder of Chautauqua Assembly at the Sunday evening vesper services in the Hall of Philosophy hold up the worthy example of Howard Arnold Walter, and quote his immortal lines to give wings to his words.

Young people are fond of singing these words in their devotional meetings, or when assembled in conventions. A persistent memory remains of a summer evening in the lovely Sage Chapel in East Northfield, Massachusetts. Representatives of the Society of Christian Endeavor were holding a summer conference extending over several days. On this particular evening a public meeting was held, and the delegations responded to roll call of communities which they represented. Sometimes a single member of a group would be chosen to render a solo, or to recite some lines. Each delegation made its own plans for representation. But probably the most impressive feature of the evening came when a body of young men went to the front of the Chapel to represent a particular society. Their ages ran from the advanced teens to about twenty-five.

The audience which crowded the beautiful building seemed to be deeply moved by this sight, and wondered what these young people planned to do. Soon in clear, steady voices they began to sing—

" I would be true, for there are those who trust me;
I would be pure, for there are those who care."

Prayerful desire and sturdy resolution were voiced in their song. Members of the faculty, parents, and visitors who were present, together with the other young people, were deeply moved as they listened to the successive lines from the singing lips of young men who were making their vows of purposeful living in song. When the music ended and the young people returned to their seats, it seemed to be almost a sacramental moment.

Boy's Interpretation of a Hymn

" Jesus, I live to Thee,
The loveliest and best;
My life in Thee, Thy life in me,
In Thy blest love I rest."

When Calvin Coolidge, Jr., died while his father was the President of the United States, this hymn was sung at his funeral. This is the Academy Hymn of Mercersburg, and young Coolidge was a student at Mercersburg Academy.

Speaking before the General Conference of the Methodist Episcopal Church in May, 1932, the Rev. Hugh T. Kerr, D.D., related the fact that he had been associated with the revision of the hymnal of the Presbyterian Church, and at one time became particularly interested in the Mercersburg Hymn. When, therefore, he met one of the boys of that educational institution, he began to discuss the hymn with him. The minister expressed surprise, he said, that boys should choose such a hymn, as there was something morbid about it, inasmuch as it spoke a good deal about death, especially in the second stanza:

> " Jesus, I die to Thee,
>   Whenever death shall come;
> To die in Thee is life to me
>   In my eternal home."

The minister confessed that he thought that he had spoken words of wisdom to the lad. The boy, however, arose from his chair, and there was a strange light in his eyes. Said he: " Sir, you do not understand. We don't sing about death. We sing about Jesus. You see, it is like this, we sing:

> " ' Jesus I live to Thee,
>   The loveliest and best;
> My life in Thee, Thy life in me,
>   In Thy blest love I rest.'

You see, after you have said that, nothing matters."

Then this confession was made by Dr. Kerr, as he referred to the lad being set on fire by a passion for Christ, " I thought I understood modern youth, but I didn't." The minister of wide experience and the youth approaching young manhood were interpreting the hymn in two different ways. Like Paul, the students were willing to live for Christ; but if death should come, as it did to Calvin Coolidge, Jr., then they would meet it with Christian loyalty and resignation. Therefore they could sing:

> " Whether to live or die,
>   I know not which is best;
> To live in Thee is bliss to me,
>   To die is endless rest."

At Mercersburg the boys sing this stanza (the third) softly, "and pass on into the fourth loudly and triumphantly." Thus the fourth stanza becomes for the boys a prayer, as they sing each Sunday just before the sermon these words:

> " Living or dying, Lord,
> I ask but to be Thine;
> My life in Thee, Thy life in me,
> Makes heaven forever mine."

This hymn was written in 1850, though it was not published until about 1861. The author, the Rev. Henry Harbaugh, D.D., was a minister of the German Reformed Church. He served pastorates in Pennsylvania, and later became a professor of theology.

In the Methodist Hymnal this hymn appears under the section, "The Christian Life," and the division, "Trust and Assurance." "The Hymnal" (Presbyterian) places it under "The Life in Christ" ("Dedication and Consecration"). But the youth of Mercersburg Academy, by adopting it as their school hymn, have also indicated that it is an acceptable song for young people.

" Fairest Lord Jesus "

> " Fairest Lord Jesus
> Ruler of all nature,
> O Thou of God and man the Son,
> Thee will I cherish,
> Thee will I honor,
> Thee, my soul's Glory, Joy, and Crown.

> " Fair are the meadows,
> Fairer still the woodlands,
> Robed in the blooming garb of spring:

Jesus is fairer,
Jesus is purer,
Who makes the woeful heart to sing."

Unexpected circumstances found me in Brooklyn during Eastertide, 1930. Therefore on Easter morning, April 20, I joined the crowd of ten thousand people of all ages who gathered for the Easter Dawn Service at Prospect Park Plaza. The chilly morning, somewhat cloudy, soon developed into a warm, cloudless day—a perfect Easter Sunday.

Participating in the music that morning were the Salvation Army Band, the Gloria Trumpeters, and the Sunset Park Choral Society. The assembled audience formed a mighty chorus; for all seemed to be in the singing mood, and we were supplied with the words of the hymns on the programs which were distributed.

Among the Easter hymns there was included the "Crusaders' Hymn," with its long history, "Fairest Lord Jesus," which was sung to its lilting tune, so familiar to American congregations. The Park facing us, with all the freshness of springtime, together with bursting buds and opening flowers, gave emphasis to the line,

"Robed in the blooming garb of spring."

Young people are attracted to this song, and compilers usually include it in the hymn books arranged for them. Charles Arthur Boyd says ("Stories of Hymns for Creative Living"): "This is one of the prized lyric legacies from the distant past. It praises Christ so joyously and sincerely that it is no wonder it is in every generation a favorite hymn."

Life's Turning-Point

" How does a man get your kind of religion? " a young Cornishman asked his employer. The younger man had been impressed by the consistent conduct of the older one.

" I came to Jesus as I was," replied his employer, as he quoted a line from one of the well-known hymns.

Soon afterward the young man attended a religious service, and, after the minister had preached on the text, " Come unto Me," the congregation sang a hymn which contained the words which he had heard from the lips of his employer. That night the youth decided to accept the great invitation. He related the incident when at Bradford, in 1937, he was one of eighty ministers ordained by the Methodist Conference; and he indicated that the words of a hymn changed the whole course of his life.

The Rev. Horatius Bonar, D.D., born at Edinburgh, 1808, was one of Scotland's foremost hymn writers, and this is " probably the most widely known and best loved of the many fine hymns " which the distinguished author wrote. Thus runs the first stanza, which portrays the individual's relation to Christ:

> " I heard the voice of Jesus say,
> ' Come unto me and rest;
> Lay down, thou weary one, lay down
> Thy head upon my breast.'
> I came to Jesus as I was,
> Weary and worn and sad;
> I found in Him a resting place,
> And He has made me glad."

This discriminating note has been made by W. T. Stead: " It belongs to the number of those [hymns] in which the converted recite their experiences for the encouragement of the unconverted. The persistent use of ' I ' and ' me ' in this hymn has helped it to help many to whom ' we ' and ' us ' would have been much less effective."

Song Selected by Young Preachers

A group of young ministers attending a summer school of ministerial training with which the writer was at that time associated, expressed a desire for a School Song. These young preachers ranged in age from about twenty to somewhat over thirty. The officers of the school suggested that the students make their own selection for that purpose, and meantime wondered what the choice might be. The students discussed the merits and appropriateness of several hymns, and eventually reported that they had decided on the virile hymn of Dr. Maltbie D. Babcock—

> " Be strong!
> We are not here to play, to dream, to drift:
> We have hard work to do and loads to lift;
> Shun not the struggle: face it—'tis God's gift."

" This is a strenuous hymn," someone has said. Probably that is why it was chosen by the young ministers. They were meeting the daily challenge of a ministry in town and country. Close observers were they of daily life. Something of the heroic was, perhaps unconsciously, displayed in their daily activities. Leaders were they of community causes. Already they had begun to realize something of the demands which would be made on them during the oncoming years.

Returning to the summer school year after year, they

and their successors in the student body continued to sing:

> "Be strong!
> It matters not how deep entrenched the wrong,
> How hard the battle goes, the day, how long;
> Faint not, fight on! Tomorrow comes the song."

Determination was seen in their faces, and prayerful courage was in their hearts, as their voices heroically voiced the words, "Be strong!"

The writer of this hymn, born in Syracuse, New York, graduated from Syracuse University in 1879. Not only did he take high rank as a student, but also as a musician and an athlete. "He was leader of the glee club, director of the orchestra, active on the baseball team, a participant in all kinds of outdoor life, and at the same time an earnest and effective worker in religious activities. He had an agile mind and a magnetic personality." He was characterized as being "tall, broad-shouldered, with muscles of steel." Following his graduation from Auburn Theological Seminary, he became one of the best known Presbyterian ministers in the country. At the early age of forty-three he died in the International Hospital, Naples, Italy (May 18, 1901), while making a foreign trip.

Fifty years after his graduation from Syracuse University, the hymn of this beloved alumnus was sung during the commencement. The writer was present on that occasion. A thousand young men and women of the graduating class were joined by four thousand others—members of the faculty, graduates, undergraduates and visitors—in singing, "Be Strong." Chancellor Charles W. Flint (later Bishop Flint) made reference in his baccalaureate sermon to the "vigorous qualities of this rugged hymn," which Bishop H. W. Warren once said was " knotted like the muscles of a torso of Hercules."

Wisely had the young ministers, therefore, chosen their summer school hymn.

CHAPTER XVII

SONGS OF MANHOOD

" Joyful, joyful, we adore Thee,
God of glory, Lord of love.

.   .   .   .   .   .

Ever singing, march we onward,
Victors in the midst of strife;
Joyful music leads us sunward
In the triumph song of life."
—*Henry van Dyke.*

The influence of his father's favorite hymn upon his own life
was once described by John H. Finley, then president of Hunter
College, and later editor of *The New York Times,* as he said:
" In a humble home of sod, set in the vast prairies of the Middle
West, by candle-light he would sing,

" ' I'm a pilgrim, I'm a stranger.'

Wistful it was, but joyful too, for it envisaged a city of perma-
nence and peace—the goal of life."—*Dr. Armstrong Stanley
Hunter.*

The Congress was 150 years old last week, and Franklin D.
Roosevelt, as President, was six. He went to his front-row pew
in St. John's Church, where the rector, Oliver J. Hart, conducted
a special anniversary service.

During the prayer President Roosevelt looked rapt in thought,
but during the hymns ("O God, Our Help in Ages Past " and
" A Mighty Fortress Is Our God ") his fine baritone could be
heard clear and confident above the male choir. *(Condensed from
" Time," March 13, 1939.)*

201

" Forth in Thy name, O Lord, I go,
My daily labor to pursue,
Thee, only Thee, resolved to know
In all I think, or speak, or do."
        —*Charles Wesley.*

" John McNeill, the Scotch evangelist, used to hear his father repeat the first verse of this hymn by Charles Wesley with his hand on the latch of the door, as he set out for his work in the quarry shortly after five in the morning."—*The Rev. John Telford.*

Business Man's Hymn

" I am not likely to forget the thrill I experienced," said a business man in England, " when I first read the words of the hymn—

> " ' Behold us, Lord, a little space
> From daily cares set free,
> And met within Thy holy place
> To rest a while with Thee.' "

This particular business man was a local preacher. He had just finished the preparation of a sermon, he said, on the text, " And whatsoever ye do, do it heartily, as to the Lord, and not unto men " (Col. 3: 23). His subject was " The Consecration of Labor."

" I was spending an hour or two selecting suitable hymns (time well spent, surely!), when my attention was attracted by the first lines of the hymn." But " the thrill came," he admitted, when he read:

> " Around us rolls the ceaseless tide
> Of business, toil, and care,
> And scarcely can we turn aside
> For one brief hour of prayer.

> " Yet these are not the only walls
> Wherein Thou mayst be sought:
> On homeliest work Thy blessing falls,
> In truth and patience wrought."

Impressed by the fact that we may glorify God by our daily toil, this business man of Sheffield added: " Every morning since then as I go to business, coming in sight of the chimneys of the small factory for the management of which I am responsible, I repeat these words to myself, and am happy to know that in ' the trivial round, the common task' we may find ' a road to lead us daily nearer God.' "

This hymn was written by John Ellerton, a clergyman in the Church of England, and was " one of the first of the hymns to recognize art and science as a part of God's work." It was composed in 1870 for " Mid-day Service in a city church." " The Hymnal " of the Episcopal Church, therefore, has it placed most appropriately under noontide hymns.

Philosopher's Favorite Hymn

Professor Borden P. Bowne, the great philosopher of Boston University, gave a generation of service in teaching before he departed this life on April 1st, 1910. This influential teacher and fruitful writer was a devoted Christian, and often found his way to the prayer meeting of his church. One of his pastors said that during the meeting he " seldom failed to express some pertinent and helpful thought." One of his favorite quotations, " given with the utmost sympathy and understanding," was from the hymn of Richard Baxter, from which he would sometimes quote two or three stanzas:

> " Lord, it belongs not to my care
> Whether I die or live;
> To love and serve Thee is my share,
> And this Thy grace must give."

He was particularly devoted to the third stanza:

> " Christ leads me through no darker rooms
> Than He went through before;
> He that into God's kingdom comes
> Must enter by this door."

Both Telford and also McCutchan, in their respective comments on this hymn, tell us that it was frequently quoted during his last illness by James Clark Maxwell, Professor of Experimental Physics at Cambridge University. This scholar gave utterance to these remarkable words: " I think men of science as well as other men need to learn from Christ, and I think Christians whose minds are scientific are bound to study science that their view of the glory of God may be as extensive as their being is capable of."

Thus the philosopher and the scientist, natives of different countries, felt the appeal to the soul of the hymn of Richard Baxter, author of " The Saints' Everlasting Rest," who lived a troubled life, but who knew the secret of inner peace, and who was submissive to the will of God. Said he in this hymn we are discussing:

> " If life be long, I will be glad,
> That I may long obey;
> If short, yet why should I be sad
> To soar to endless day? "

Astronomer's Beloved Hymn

When a student in Princeton University Dr. Robert E. Speer heard a vesper address by one whom he characterized as the " greatest astronomer in America." Relating the incident thirty years after, Dr. Speer said concerning the speaker of that distant day (whom he did not name):

" He knew more about the sun than any other living man. There were few who had seen more than he had seen. He was telling us in his simple way, so childlike and gentle, of all that Christ was to him, and then he asked us to sing his favorite hymn. What do you think was the favorite hymn of this man whose eyes had seen more in this universe than those of any other man? "

One can easily understand that the selection was a surprise to many of the students who had listened to the famous speaker of that day. The hymn which the astronomer loved was written by Dr. Ray Palmer, author of " My Faith Looks Up to Thee," and first appeared in 1858—

> " Jesus, these eyes have never seen
> That radiant form of Thine;
> The veil of sense hangs dark between
> Thy blessed face and mine.

> " I see Thee not, I hear Thee not,
> Yet Thou art oft with me;
> And earth has ne'er so dear a spot
> As when I meet with Thee."

The author, a Congregational minister, ranks with the foremost of the hymn writers of America. This hymn undoubtedly stands next among his writings to the hymn by which he became best known. When questioned by compilers concerning his preferences, he would modestly call attention to this composition. It may be found in " The Hymnal " (Presbyterian); and in the " Inter-Church Hymnal," where hymns are listed in the order of their popularity in American churches, it stands as number 286.

The day before he died, when extremely feeble, the author was overheard to repeat the closing stanza of this hymn. Thus there were with him to the last his own words—

> " When death these mortal eyes shall seal,
> And still this throbbing heart,
> The rending veil shall Thee reveal,
> All-glorious as Thou art."

Song of Daniel's Band

> " Standing by a purpose true,
> Heeding God's command,
> Honor them, the faithful few!
> All hail to Daniel's Band.

> " Dare to be a Daniel!
> Dare to stand alone!
> Dare to have a purpose firm!
> Dare to make it known!"

This sacred song belongs to the latter part of the last century, and both words and music came from Mr. Philip P. Bliss. Mr. Ira D. Sankey says: " Mr. Bliss wrote this song especially for his Sunday-school class in the First Congregational Church of Chicago. It has been much admired and was often used by me in connection with Mr. Moody's lecture on Daniel."

Yet it still makes an appeal and brings a challenge to manhood fighting its battles with temptation. An English minister, the Rev. Fred Barrett, writing from the region of the Black Country in Staffordshire in October, 1938, told the story of an organization of " Daniel's Band " in the community where he lived. Several years ago a man who had become a drunkard experienced a change of heart and life. He then wanted to share the life of happiness which he now enjoyed with others. He knew where and when to find his old pals, and one by one he won many of them for Christ.

The custom of those men had been to walk round the public market on Saturday nights, and call at the various public houses for the beverages which intoxicate. After several of them experienced the change in their lives they still met and had their walk on Saturdays, but they would now end up in a coffee house.

They were offered the use of a room in connection with one of the churches. Because they still had to meet temptation, and sometimes stand alone, they called themselves the " Daniel's Band "; and adopted the song, which they changed to suit their needs, as their rallying song.

Only men who had known the force of temptation and habit as those men had done could sing with a yearning desire:

> " Dare to be a Daniel!
> Dare to stand alone!
> Dare to pass a public house
> And take your money home! "

Surely their wives and children appreciated the significance of the last line, in which the men pledged themselves to take their money home on pay day, instead of spending it in the saloon.

When the Men's Class Sang

Amid the chill of a Thursday afternoon in mid-November, 1937, the genial editor of *The British Weekly*, Dr. John A. Hutton, went forth to fulfill an engagement in the North of London. This scholarly clergyman-editor, who has often been enthusiastically welcomed at East Northfield, Massachusetts, at its summer conferences, writing of the incident, said that for many years he had been " in regular and happy contact with the ' people called Methodists.' " Hence he was journeying for the purpose of preaching the afternoon sermon in a " fine old church (The Prince of Wales Road Church) which sixty years earlier ministered to a large middle-class congregation." Now it was adapting itself to a changed condition by serving along the lines of a modern mission. Arriving for the service, Dr. Hutton found the building filled with more than five hundred people who had come with " happy expectations."

The occasion followed the usual order of such a celebration. First, the preaching service; and this was followed by the tea-meeting, an almost indispensable part of any church anniversary occasion in England. The platform meeting came in the evening, and Dr. Hutton was also among the speakers for this gathering. These evening meetings are quite informal, usually, and tend to cultivate a warm social spirit. But on this occasion the minister, the Rev. J. R. Peacock, did something which immensely pleased the observing editor. Said Dr. Hutton, as he later described the feature: " He called upon various groups, beginning with young people, and ending with his Men's Class, and these severally sang a chorus which was a portion of a hymn. In each case the tone and volume of the voices were different; but in every case it was genuine and contagious praise."

Confessing that he was greatly stirred by the singing, Dr. Hutton added: " When the Men's Class arose and sang, I was moved as I have not been for many a day. There were some fifty of them, I should say." They sang:

" From sinking sand He lifted me;
    With tender hand He lifted me;
    From shades of night to plains of light,
    O praise His name, He lifted me! "

They were singing the chorus of the song written by Charles H. Gabriel, and which is included in the Methodist Hymn Book (London) under " The Gospel Call." Thus the hymn begins:

" In loving-kindness Jesus came,
    My soul in mercy to reclaim,
    And from the depths of sin and shame
    Through grace He lifted me."

" As I looked at those men," said Dr. Hutton, " as I listened to them, as I saw the glow mounting in their faces and betraying itself in their deepening passion of gratitude, I felt once again, Here is the true Christian apologetic."

Then, for his own gratification, as he confessed, he reprinted the first stanza of the hymn in his own editorial columns.

Another report of this service said concerning the singing by the men, " Led by one good voice, they raised a great chorus, and enjoyed it."

" One More Day's Work "

The closing moments of an Annual Conference in the Methodist Church were approaching. Business had been completed, committees had all reported, and the resolutions of appreciation had been read. Soon the presiding bishop would read the appointments, and a hundred and forty preachers would enter on a new year of ministry.

Some would begin their first year of active service, and a
few their last. Several would be changed to new appointments. Suspense (and sometimes surprise) characterizes
the closing of such a gathering.

Great care is usually exercised in the selection of an appropriate hymn for this occasion. This time, however, the
hymn chosen was one which is not often heard when a
Methodist Conference closes. At least, this is the only
time the writer recalls its use. Yet it was tenderly touching:

> " One more day's work for Jesus,
>   One less of life for me!
>   But heaven is nearer,
>   And Christ is dearer
> Than yesterday to me."

Ministers, young and old, active and retired, enthusiastically blended their voices in these words of Anna Bart-
lett Warner. Ready were these messengers of the cross to
go forth with gladness to tell the old, old story of the
love of Christ for humanity. Perhaps some of them even
recalled the suggestion which prompted Miss Warner to
write the hymn. The Rev. Benjamin M. Adams wrote a
letter at the close of a day of great activity in which he
mentioned the fact that he was physically weary, yet he
was conscious of " abounding spiritual joy." Well did
Miss Warner express the minister's thought as she wrote,

> " Lord, if I may,
>   I'll serve another day."

Within less than an hour after singing this hymn, most
of those ministers were headed for home and another
year of service. Deep in their hearts was the memory of
the song they had so recently sung.

CHAPTER XVIII

SINGING AMERICANS

" We sing our country's anthem as a pledge that we are one,
In the dream of future glories, and the struggle we have won,
And our race goes bravely forward, head-erect and clean and
    strong—
In the fellowship of music, and the Brotherhood of song."
—Edgar A. Guest.

" My country, 'tis of thee,
Sweet land of liberty,
Of thee I sing."

" In the days of peace and prosperity, through the crisis of the
Civil War, and on most public occasions since the war, this
hymn (America) has gradually won recognition as a national
one without the ceremonial of adoption in any historic scene."
—W. T. Stead.

" The first public use of the hymn (America) was at a children's celebration of Fourth of July, in 1832, in the famous Park
Street Church, Boston."—Charles A. Boyd.

" America! America! "

Citizenship in the United States cannot be bought, but must be earned, a Supreme Court Justice told a group of men and women who had just been admitted to the privileges of citizenship. They had been thoroughly trained for their new duties and responsibilities, and also prepared for their examinations, by several patriotic persons, following a method which had been in operation for several years, by a group of patriotic persons living in one of the upstate cities of New York State.

The happy occasion was publicly celebrated when more than a hundred of these new citizens came together for a banquet. With them were members of the Americanization Council, various city officials, and other persons prominent in the life of the city. Following the joyous feast, the new citizens received their naturalization papers, each in a separate envelope. To each was also presented an American flag, the gift of the widow of an editor whose husband, more than two decades earlier, had begun this labor of love of training immigrants who desired to qualify for citizenship.

These new citizens had come from Italy, Poland, Germany, Wales, England, Ireland, and many other countries. But that eventful night they shared a common thrill of happiness as they sang the lovely song of Kathrine Lee Bates:

> " O beautiful for spacious skies,
> For amber waves of grain,
> For purple mountain majesties
> Above the fruited plain! "

Radiant were the faces of those men and women as they

sang with joyful emotion words which to them were a
sacred prayer for the land of their adoption—

> "America! America!
> God shed His grace on thee,
> And crown thy good with brotherhood
> From sea to shining sea."

Sharing a common happiness and a spirit of patriotism,
the occasion was for all present a sacramental moment of
sacred dedication to America's highest welfare.

Colored Citizen Sang "The Battle Hymn of the Republic"

The dedication of the New York State Roosevelt Memorial occurred on January 19, 1936. This is located near
the American Museum of Natural History in New York
City, and Mr. A. Perry Osborn, a trustee, accepted the
building on behalf of the museum, with a pledge to keep
the Roosevelt Memorial sacred to "the ideals of Theodore
Roosevelt."

Colonel Roosevelt, a son of the one-time President of
the United States, in speaking, revealed the fact that his
father had told him that there had been a time in his life
when he almost decided to become a professional natural-
ist. He also stated that throughout his father's entire life
natural history was always his "greatest loved avocation."

Such a ceremony of dedication would not be complete
without music in some form. What, considering all the
circumstances, could be more appropriate for such an occasion than the song,

"Mine eyes have seen the glory of the coming of the Lord"?

Reporting the event, *The New York Times* said the next day, " Roland Hayes, the Negro tenor, sang ' The Battle Hymn of the Republic ' so magnificently that he was called to the front of the stage twice to acknowledge the applause."

Thus a colored man, representing a race which had come into the heritage of freedom, sang at a memorial for the great President of the United States who had been the friend of humanity, white and black alike, the song written by a woman who had done much, by her pen, for the liberation of those who once were in bondage. Once again did men and women hear the thrilling lines of Julia Ward Howe:

" In the beauty of the lilies Christ was born across the sea,
With a glory in His bosom that transfigures you and me;
As He died to make men holy, let us die to make them free,
While God is marching on."

" America " Heard Around the World

" My country, 'tis of thee,
Sweet land of liberty,
Of thee I sing."

Conducted in Washington, D. C., and participated in by President Herbert Hoover, the exercises in connection with the bi-centennial of George Washington (February 22, 1932) were heard around the world. On that occasion, when the signal was given by President Hoover at the Capitol, more than ten thousand persons in the open air joined in singing " America " under the direction of Walter Damrosch. Two thousand of these were school children, assembled for the occasion. The Marine, Army and

Navy Bands were massed, and, directed by John Philip Sousa, accompanied the singers.

To every part of America, and also to other countries, the exercises were conveyed by radio. Thousands of homes and gatherings assembled in various places for the occasion were thrilled as the radio brought to them the song of Samuel F. Smith. The country joined in its tribute to the Father of his Country. Clearly the words were heard, and they awakened a responsive echo in the hearts of Americans everywhere—

> " Our fathers' God to Thee,
> Author of liberty,
>   To Thee we sing:
> Long may our land be bright
> With freedom's holy light;
> Protect us by Thy might,
>   Great God our King."

Singing " America " with Streaming Eyes

During the closing weeks of the Civil War, Secretary Stanton wired Henry Ward Beecher after every important development. This influential preacher, pastor of Plymouth Church, Brooklyn, gave himself unsparingly in the interest of the Union cause. Lyman Beecher Stowe has preserved for us the following incident:

" On Sunday morning, April 2, 1865, in Plymouth Church, just after the sermon, a telegram from Secretary Stanton was handed to Beecher in the pulpit announcing decisive Union victories after three days of hard fighting. After reading it aloud Beecher asked the thousand present to turn to ' America.' The great company, realizing that the war was practically over, sang the noble anthem with streaming eyes."

Profoundly deep must have been the impression as the mighty volume of voices rang out the reverent lines:

> " Our fathers' God, to Thee,
> Author of liberty,
> To Thee we sing."

Singing at the Sight of " Old Glory "

The power of patriotic song was forcefully illustrated on July 1st, 1898, on the ramparts of Santiago. Man after man belonging to the Twenty-first regulars was falling before the blazing fire of Mauser bullets. Then, at a critical moment, the soldiers caught a fresh gleam of the Stars and Stripes. Spontaneously they began to sing:

> " Oh, say, does that star-spangled banner yet wave
> O'er the land of the free and the home of the brave? "

It was a song in season. Colonel Nicholas Smith in relating the incident says that the majestic strains of " The Star-Spangled Banner " so stirred and " thrilled the souls of the men that they seemed to be nerved by some superhuman power to defy the storm of battle, and to win the victory that sealed the fate of Santiago."

Negro Band Played " The Star-Spangled Banner " in France

> " Oh, say, can you see, by the dawn's early light,
> What so proudly we hailed at the twilight's last gleaming?
> Whose broad stripes and bright stars, thro' the perilous fight,

O'er the ramparts we watched, were so gallantly streaming?
And the rockets' red glare, the bombs bursting in air,
Gave proof thro' the night that our flag was still there.

" Oh, say, does that star-spangled banner yet wave
   O'er the land of the free and the home of the brave? "

Having been a student in Syracuse University, Lieu-
tenant Sidman Poole sent a letter to *The Syracusan*
(which was published in 1919) giving his experience in
France, where he served in the World War, on Memorial
Day. Said the writer:

" Memorial Day in France! And I doubt whether I shall
ever see another as impressive as this. Perhaps I was
nearer to its real meaning than ever before.

" In the American Cemetery at Nantes there are perhaps four hundred graves. Twelve months ago there were
none.

" Several thousand people were at the cemetery for the
service at 10 A. M. today. There was a detachment of
marines and horizon-blue clad French soldiers. A negro
band played ' America ' and ' Nearer, My God, to Thee.'
Colonel Knudson gave an address, as did also a French
general. Then an army chaplain offered prayer.

" Over the graves were fired three volleys; then the
beautiful notes of ' Taps ' floated out. The band crashed
out ' The Star-Spangled Banner,' the colors were uncased,
and the flag slowly raised to the peak. That was all—
short but impressive. Soldiers, nurses, and hundreds of
French civilians looked on during the exercises."